D0927502

MIDI for Musicians

by Craig Anderton.

MIDI for Musicians.

by Craig Anderton.

&

Amsco Publications.
New York/London/Sydney

Interior design and layout by The Bookmakers, Incorporated.

Copyright © 1986 by Amsco Publications,
A Division of Music Sales Corporation, New York, NY.

All rights reserved. No part of this book may be
reproduced in any form or by any electronic or mechanical means
including information storage and retrieval systems,
without permission in writing from the publisher,
except by a reviewer who may quote brief passages in a review.

Order No. AM 61219
International Standard Book Number: 0.8256.1050.8

Exclusive Distributors:
Music Sales Corporation
257 Park Avenue South, New York, NY 10010 USA
Music Sales Limited
8/9 Frith Street, London W1V 5TZ England
Music Sales Pty. Limited
120 Rothschild Street, Rosebery, Sydney, NSW 2018, Australia

Printed in the United States of America by
Vicks Lithograph and Printing Corporation

Contents

Foreword

MIDI IS FAB! At last, a system that enables our keyboards to talk to each other. I remember the virtually orgasmic experience of first hearing the layered textures of my Prophet T-8 and two DX-7s linked via MIDI. Live work is streamlined with a master MIDI keyboard linked up to a synth module (no need for bulky keyboards) located tidily off stage. Now with reverb machines, sequencers, drum machines, and industrial compressors all receptive to much MIDI info . . . well, what can I say?

I'm sure you will enjoy finding out more of the possibilities of MIDI in Craig's book *MIDI for Musicians.*

Howard Jones

Preface

The first time I played with MIDI, it gave me the same creative rush as when I laid down an overdub on my first multitrack tape recorder. MIDI is great fun; it opens up many new possibilities for musicians. But to get the most out of MIDI, you'll need some solid background information—and that's the point of this book.

MIDI makes a lot more sense when you know why it was necessary. So Chapter 1 covers the evolution toward MIDI—including how musicians got equipment to work together in the pre-MIDI days. MIDI is also heavily dependent on computers, so Chapter 2 demystifies the topic of computers in music. Chapters 3 and 4 cover the MIDI "language." Once you're equipped with all this theory, it's time to get into applications—from how to evaluate whether a particular piece of MIDI gear is going to serve your needs or not (Chapter 5), to MIDI's musical uses (Chapter 6), and finally to the MIDI sequencer-based recording studio (Chapter 7). Chapter 8 covers popular MIDI accessories, and Chapter 9 speculates about what MIDI will bring us in the months and years to come. Supplementary, more technical information is presented as sidebar information when appropriate.

MIDI is in a constant state of flux, and new MIDI products are invented on a seem-ingly daily basis. As a result, there's no way that a book can cover "everything there is to know about MIDI." It's an impossible task since some genius in a garage somewhere is probably coming up with a MIDI kazoo controller even as I'm writing this. No matter. The most important part of learning about MIDI is to know enough to understand MIDI specifications. Once you know the MIDI language, you'll be able to make the right purchasing decisions, choose compatible equipment, apply products properly, squeeze the last ounce of performance out of the equipment you have, and generally have a good time no matter what new gear comes out in the future.

I spent quite some time being frustrated and impatient before I finally got MIDI sorted out, but the effort was worth it. It's also going to take you a while to get through this book; MIDI cannot be learned in a day . . . so be patient. When you're finished, you'll have a firm understanding of a musical development which is just as significant—if not more so—as synthesizers and multitrack recorders.

Enjoy! If you have even half as much fun as I've had playing with MIDI, you're in for a real good time.

Acknowledgments

Many people and companies helped me with this book. I would like to thank Akai, Casio, E-mu, Passport Designs, Roland, and Syntech for the use of their equipment so that I could hook lots of different devices together. I am grateful to Sequential, Yamaha, Simmons, and Key Clique for providing me with documentation on their equipment. Also thanks to Bill Godbout at Viasyn/CompuPro for hot-rodding my computer so that it's the fastest word processor I've ever used.

Thank yous are in order to three people who graciously consented to look over this book for possible errors so that I wouldn't make a fool of myself in public. These are J. L. Cooper, who knows just about all there is to know about getting MIDI (and non-MIDI) equipment to work together reliably; Vanessa Else, Assistant Editor at *Electronic Musician* magazine, who helped clean up some of my English and also proofed the manuscript for continuity; and Jim Wright (a co-developer of Octave-Plateau's Sequencer Plus program), whose seminal "What MIDI Means to Musicians" article was the Rosetta stone to many budding MIDI fanatics (myself included). His MIDI expertise, his generosity in sharing his knowledge, and his enthusiasm for this project were invaluable and greatly appreciated.

Thanks to the Roland Corporation for letting me use the title *MIDI for Musicians,* even though they had copyrighted that title for a previously published pamphlet of theirs. I would like to add that Roland has been very conscientious about educating musicians on the subject of MIDI; they sponsor seminars around the country on MIDI applications and offer instructional materials such as booklets and tapes.

Thank you to Howard Jones, who was kind enough to say "yes" when asked if he'd care to write a few words for the foreword; to Frank Serafine, for taking the time to really explain MIDI studios to me; to *Electronic Musician, Output,* and *Musician* magazines for permission to reprint portions of articles I had written for them; to John Simonton (president, Synchronous Technologies) and Terry Fryer for helping me with the section on sequencer sync-to-tape using SMPTE; to Donna Murray at E-mu for being incredibly patient when I kept asking stupid MIDI questions; to Larry Fast (Peter Gabriel band), Paul Lehrman (Southworth Music Systems), and Bobby Nathan (Unique Recording) for additional technical advice; and to all the people who said "so you're writing a MIDI book—well, did you know that . . ." and therefore gave me even more things to think about.

And while I'm getting all teary-eyed here, one more thing. MIDI to me represents a very positive political statement. MIDI was the result of a joint effort by many rival companies and engineers, from Japan and the U.S. alike, who were able to shelve their differences and get on with the important work of making better tools for musicians. Egos had to be restrained; companies had to learn how to work together; and many issues had to be resolved. Yet those in the music industry somehow persevered and, as a result of their collaboration, created something truly important. In so doing, they avoided the mistake that home computer, video disk, and VCR manufacturers made when they couldn't agree on common specifications. This book, then, is gratefully dedicated to the people who made MIDI a reality.

Chapter 1

The Evolution toward MIDI

What's a MIDI?

MIDI stands for *Musical Instrument Digital Interface.* You already know what *musical instrument* means, so that takes care of the first part. *Digital* means that information (data) about the musical instrument is conveyed in digital, or computer-based, language. *Interface* is the term for the actual link between instruments, where data passes from one instrument to another. So, MIDI is a link between those musical instruments capable of transmitting and receiving computer data. MIDI's purpose is to allow electronic musical instruments from different manufacturers to work together as an efficient music-making system.

About This Chapter

MIDI didn't just happen by accident; it was a carefully thought-out response to some of the problems that were occurring with electronic musical instruments. To understand MIDI, it helps to understand the musical evolution that led to MIDI and the problems that MIDI solves. *Once you fully understand why MIDI was necessary, the whole concept makes a lot more sense.*

Much of this first chapter explains how synthesizers were made to work together in the pre-MIDI world. You might wonder why we're bothering to go over "obsolete" information, but absorbing this background will give you a stable, solid foundation for learning about MIDI. Also, it will allow you to use older equipment in a MIDI system. Hang in there; we'll get to MIDI itself in due time.

Voltage Control: The First Synthesizer Instrument Interface

Please note: This section is the most difficult part of the whole book. If you have a hard

time dealing with it, just absorb as much as you can and proceed to the next section ("Some Other Problems from the Early Days of Synthesizers"). The main point we're trying to get across is that MIDI is built on what has come before but offers numerous advantages over the pre-MIDI way of doing things.

Soon after synthesizers were introduced, it became clear that this new technology created problems as well as solved them. Perhaps most seriously from a musician's standpoint, analog synthesizers tended to sound "thin" compared to traditional acoustic instruments, which have very complex timbres. In addition, many synthesizers were *monophonic* (capable of creating only one sound at a time). This frustrated keyboard players, who were naturally accustomed to playing chords.

One remedy was to play two monophonic synthesizers simultaneously—one with the left hand and one with the right. Playing unison lines or two-note harmonies created a much thicker sound than a single synthesizer, but unfortunately having both hands occupied meant that you couldn't manipulate any of the synth's knobs or modulation wheels while playing.

The next evolutionary step was to "slave" two monophonic synthesizers together *electronically* so that as you played on one synth keyboard the other synth would follow along and play the same notes. To explain how this works, we need to understand the concept of *voltage control.*

When you play a traditional synthesizer keyboard, you are not actually playing notes from the keyboard in the sense of a piano, where a hammer strikes a string; rather, pressing each key sends a *voltage* to the synthesizer's *voltage-controlled oscillator* (VCO for short). A VCO is a tone generator whose pitch is determined by the amount of voltage

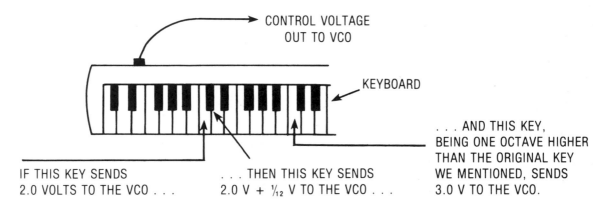

CONTROL VOLTAGE
OUT TO VCO

KEYBOARD

... AND THIS KEY,
BEING ONE OCTAVE HIGHER
THAN THE ORIGINAL KEY
WE MENTIONED, SENDS
3.0 V TO THE VCO.

IF THIS KEY SENDS
2.0 VOLTS TO THE VCO . . .

. . . THEN THIS KEY SENDS
2.0 V + $\frac{1}{12}$ V TO THE VCO . . .

Figure 1–1

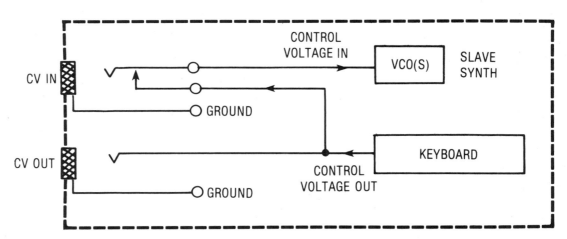

WITH NOTHING PLUGGED INTO THE SLAVE SYNTH'S "CONTROL VOLTAGE IN" JACK,
THE SWITCHING CONTACT CONNECTS THE KEYBOARD'S CONTROL VOLTAGE OUTPUT
TO THE VCO OR VCOS.

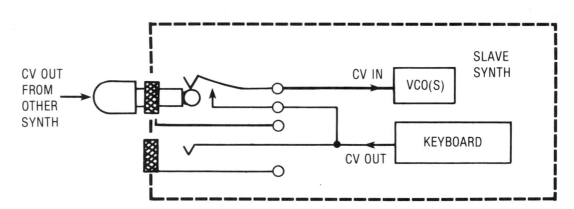

WITH A PLUG INSERTED INTO THE SLAVE SYNTH'S "CONTROL VOLTAGE IN" JACK,
THE SWITCHING CONTACT INTERRUPTS THE KEYBOARD VOLTAGE GOING TO THE VCO.
THE CONTROL VOLTAGE CONNECTED TO THE PLUG NOW GOES TO THE SLAVE SYNTH'S VCO(S).

Figure 1–2

feeding into its *control voltage input*. Therefore, playing different keys sends out different voltages to the VCO, which interprets these voltages as different pitches. Most VCOs follow a *1 volt (V) per octave* response, meaning that the VCO pitch doubles every time the control voltage increases by 1 V. For example, suppose playing a particular key sends 1 V to the VCO. Then playing 1 octave higher on the keyboard sends out 2 V to the VCO. If you play yet another octave higher, the keyboard will send out 3V to the VCO. With this 1 V per octave response, each key generates $1/12$ V (since there are 12 notes per octave) more than the key below it and $1/12$ V less than the key above it (see **Fig. 1-1**).

Got that? If not, don't worry . . . just keep reading because all this information is now going to be put to some practical use.

Suppose we take the keyboard's control voltage output and feed it to *two* VCOs (oscillators) at once. As long as they both have a 1 V per octave response, the keyboard will control both of them simultaneously. Aha! Now we have a single keyboard driving two oscillators at once, thereby producing a thicker sound. In fact, inside most synthesizers two or even more oscillators are controlled from the keyboard control voltage.

So how do we slave two synthesizers together? First, the "master" synth (Synth 1) must have a *control voltage output jack* that sends (outputs) the control voltage generated by the keyboard. Second, the "slave" synth (Synth 2) must have a *control voltage input jack* that receives (inputs) this voltage. Typically, plugging into the control voltage input jack disconnects the slave's oscillators from its own keyboard, thus allowing the slave to accept the external control voltage from the master keyboard. **Fig. 1-2** shows how a *switching jack* provides this function: With nothing plugged into the jack, the switch con-

tacts route the slave's keyboard control voltage output to the slave synthesizer's oscillators. Plugging into the control voltage (CV) input jack interrupts this path and instead sends the voltage coming from the plug (connected to the master synthesizer) to the slave synthesizer's oscillators.

Fig. 1-3 shows our master/slave setup. Playing Synth 1's keyboard sends a control voltage to Synth 1's oscillators but also sends a duplicate control voltage to Synth 2's oscillators. Thus, Synth 2 will track whatever you play on Synth 1. Setting the two synthesizers for different timbres will create thick, harmonically complex sounds.

However, we're not quite finished yet since we need to make sure that the notes on both synths turn on and off together. Many people don't realize that synthesizer oscillators are generating tones *all the time*. Once you hit a key and generate a control voltage, the keyboard will keep sending out that voltage—even if you remove your finger from the key—until you hit another key, at which point the keyboard sends out the new voltage. So why don't we *hear* the oscillator tone at all times? Well, another circuit, called a *voltage controlled amplifier* (or VCA) gates the oscillator tone on and off. Like the VCO, the VCA also has a control voltage input; the VCA level is directly proportional to the voltage present at its control voltage input. For example, with a +10 V control voltage the gain would be at maximum; and lowering the voltage progressively down to 0 volts would lower the VCA gain down to minimum.

When you press down a keyboard key, in addition to sending out a control voltage to the oscillators the keyboard sends out a second signal called a *gate*. If the gate signal goes from 0 volts (key up) to +10 V (key down), we could feed the gate directly into the VCA to turn it on and off in time with

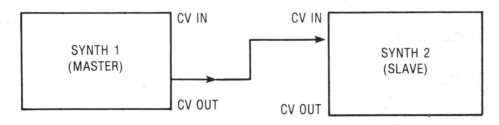

Figure 1-3

our playing. However, since simply gating a tone on and off sounds pretty uninteresting, about two decades ago Robert Moog came up with a nifty little circuit called an *envelope generator* (EG for short; see sidebar). When triggered by a gate, an EG can add dynamics (attack and decay time) to the sound by generating a control voltage that controls the VCA in a specific way.

How does this relate back to our master/slave setup? All we need to do is make sure that the master synth has a gate output and that the slave synth has a gate input. Like the switching action of the control voltage input, plugging into the gate input disconnects the slave synth's EG from its own keyboard, thus allowing the slave to accept the gate signal from the master keyboard.

Fig. 1-5 shows the final master/slave setup for two monophonic synthesizers. Playing a key on Synth 1 sends a control voltage out to the oscillators in Synth 2 and a gate signal out to the EG(s) in Synth 2. Tra-la! We now have the two synths playing together . . . well, maybe we have the two synths playing together. You see, even though we have made all the right connections, not all synthesizers follow the same control voltage and gate protocols. Yes, the ugly specter of nonstandardization is rearing its ugly head. Connecting some synthesizers together causes no problems; but if you try to slave an old Korg and Moog synthesizer together, they will not track because the Korg does not follow a 1 V per octave control voltage response. Therefore, although the notes will turn on and off together, they won't necessarily be at the same pitch. On the other hand, if you slave a Moog and ARP synthesizer together the oscillators will track; but since they do not follow the same gate protocol, the notes won't turn on and off together. (You can probably see why musicians started to feel the need for a standard synthesizer interface.)

Another problem is that this scheme will work only for monophonic synthesizers. Just when musicians were finally starting to figure out this whole control voltage/gate thing, inexpensive polyphonic synthesizers started to appear which could not be slaved together in the same manner. So, with a few exceptions, the concept of connecting instruments

together went on the back burner . . . until MIDI appeared. As we'll see later on, one of MIDI's main features is the ability to slave synthesizers together from a wide variety of manufacturers. With MIDI, note pitch and on/off information became standardized so that MIDI instruments from any two manufacturers could slave together relatively painlessly.

Envelope Generator Basics

A typical EG generates a control voltage and typically has four variable parameters: attack time, initial decay time, sustain level, and release time. Referring to **Fig. 1-4**, pressing down on a key sends a gate to the EG, which starts its attack phase. During the attack phase, which is typically adjustable to anywhere from a few milliseconds to several seconds, the EG control voltage output rises from 0 volts to maximum. Since this control voltage controls the VCA, the signal "fades in" from zero to maximum level over the specified attack time period.

During the initial decay phase, the voltage drops over an adjustable period of time from the maximum level to a variable sustain level, thus lowering the VCA level. Holding your finger down on a key maintains the sustain level (remember, as long as a key is down the gate signal continues to feed the EG). The VCA output will be louder with a high sustain level than a low sustain level.

Removing your finger from the key turns the gate off, and the EG responds by going into the release phase. During the release time, the VCA fades out from the sustain level back down to 0 gain.

So . . . let's recap. You press down a key, and this starts the attack and initial decay phases of the EG. Continuing to hold the key holds the EG at its sustain level. Releasing the key removes the gate signal, thus sending the EG into its release phase.

Some Other Problems from the Early Days of Synthesizers

Here are some other historical problems that MIDI now solves, as we'll see later on.

The redundant keyboard problem. Although slaving keyboards together worked okay, it meant that one of the keyboards was now redundant. Since the most expensive part of the synth is often the keyboard, and since every synth had a keyboard, this dupli-

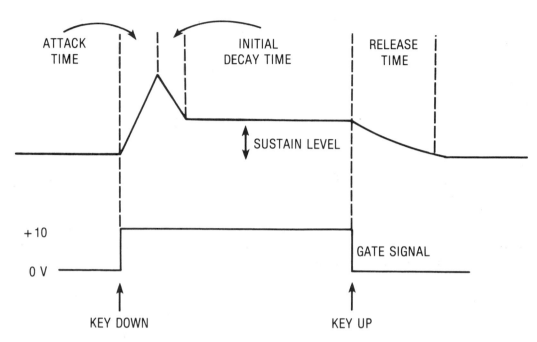

Figure 1-4

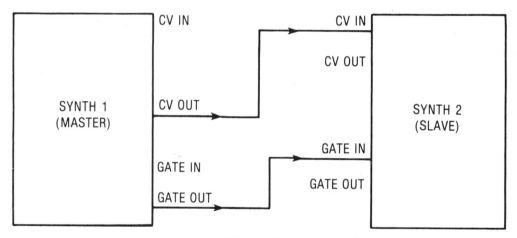

Figure 1-5

cation was financially wasteful. These multiple keyboards also created a lot of clutter.

There were two possible solutions to this problem. One was to buy a completely modular system—where the keyboard (which only put out control voltage and gate signals) was sold separately from the other modules (VCOs, VCAs, envelope generators, etc.). You could start with, say, a simple system containing a couple of oscillators and eventually pick up more modules that were driven from the original keyboard. The main problem with modular synthesizers was size and expense, since these were essentially semicustom instruments. For musicians who preferred self-contained units, such as the mini-

moog or ARP Odyssey, the only way to not have redundant keyboards was to pick up an old synth second hand, remove the keyboard, and repackage the remaining electronics into a sort of expander module. Needless to say, few musicians had the time, courage, or knowledge to gut a piece of expensive equipment in this manner.

The synchronization problem. Matters deteriorated even further when drum machines and sequencers got into the act. (Sequencers are accessory devices that "remember" which notes are played on a synthesizer, then play back those notes into the synthesizer to re-create the original performance—sort of like a high-tech player piano.)

Many times, Company A's drum machine would run at a different speed from Company B's sequencer (we'll explain why in a bit); and when the two were hooked together, it was not the best of all situations. Until MIDI came along, there never really was a simple solution to this problem, although a number of companies made adapter boxes that allowed supposedly incompatible units to enjoy a certain amount of compatibility.

Obsolescence. Due to the rapid rate of technological change, instruments often became obsolete within a few months after their introduction. Eventually keyboard players were almost afraid to buy anything because they felt that a newer, better version would be introduced soon. Although MIDI hasn't put an end to this problem, it has certainly helped extend the useful life of a piece of equipment by making it compatible with newer devices.

The problem of changing sounds rapidly. In the early days of electronic music, modular synthesizers were the only game in town. The individual modules were connected by *patch cords* in order to create a complete sound. For example, listening to the output of the oscillator itself is pretty dull; but by patching a filter into the signal path and varying the filter, you can make more interesting sounds.

During the late 60s, companies such as Moog, EMS (London), and ARP produced large, multimodule synthesizers. While capable of creating a great many sounds, they had a serious drawback: changing from one sound to another took a very long time, as patch cords had to be rerouted and dials had to be changed. In studio situations this usually wasn't too drastic a problem, but for live use having to fool with all those dials and patch cords made life very difficult.

One solution was to prepackage a bunch of modules in a box and route signals, not with patch cords, but by flicking switches or turning volume controls up or down. The minimoog was pretty much the first of these "normalized" synthesizers (so called because the internal modules had a "normal," standard configuration). It was certainly a lot easier to hit a switch or two than plug and unplug patch cords. Then there was the "Rick Wakeman Brute Force Approach,"

which involved setting up lots of synthesizers, each one set to its own patch. Although this looked pretty impressive on stage, few people could afford this kind of conspicuous consumption.

The Sequential Circuits Prophet 5, a programmable normalized synthesizer that remembered front panel control settings, elegantly solved the problem of having to reset controls and switches to obtain different sounds. Once you had diddled the knobs sufficiently to find an appealing sound, you could press a few buttons and store all the control settings in memory. From that point on, all successful synths were programmable devices.

Nonetheless, all was not yet perfect. Many keyboard players still liked to play more than one keyboard at a time, often playing one keyboard with one hand and one keyboard with the other. If you changed patches (now called *programs*) on one machine and wanted to select a suitable program on another machine, you had to select both programs individually. Although that might not be too big a deal, if you also had a drum machine and sequencer, those programs needed to change for each song. This meant a lot of button-pushing between songs . . . especially if you also had to make some changes to a delay line or equalizer. MIDI came to the rescue by letting you designate one MIDI device as the master. If you change the program on the master, all other MIDI devices (assuming they have program change capability, which not all do) will follow suit. Thus, if you select Song 26 on a drum machine, your keyboard will call up the right sound, your sequencer will find the right sequence, and your MIDI delay line will even go to the correct delay setting. Progress!

The Evolution of Synchronization

Hopefully the preceding has given you a taste of some of the problems involved in using electronic musical instruments and why MIDI was necessary. However, MIDI is designed to do far more than solve just these basic kinds of problems. In fact, one of MIDI's greatest features is its ability to rhythmically synchronize all elements in an electronic music system. Just as we had to cover some of the basics of analog synthesis in order to understand one aspect of MIDI, we now need to cover synchronization basics in order to understand a different aspect of MIDI.

With human players someone (typically a drummer) usually keeps time and the others follow that person for their timing cues. With electronic systems the timekeeper is called **a** *clock*; and when turned on (usually at the beginning of a song), it emits a steady stream of pulses. Devices such as drum machines and sequencers count the number of pulses since the clock was first started. Providing that the instruments in the system count at the same rate, if the drum machine plays a certain sound at, say, the 345th pulse and the sequencer plays another sound at the 345th pulse, you will hear the two sounds at precisely the same time.

Each clock pulse is a pulse of energy, like the tick or tock of a clock. Usually it is a square or pulse waveform (like the kind used in synthesizers but generally occurring at **a** lower frequency). Clock pulses are the electrical equivalent of a pendulum, but instead of swinging back and forth between two points, a clock pulse swings back and forth between a maximum and minimum voltage (see **Fig. 1-6**). This is a very unambiguous type of signal—it's either full on or full off. As we'll see later on, MIDI uses the same kind of *binary* (two possible states) **on** or **off** signal.

The simplest, and least successful, way to synchronize two devices is to set their respective internal clocks for the same tempo and start them at exactly the same time. Although this sounds good in theory, in practice there are several problems. First off, how do you set *exactly* the same tempo for both machines? Even if each device has a readout to indicate the tempo, there is no guarantee that the indicated readout is 100 percent accurate. The tempo can also drift, over time,

due to subtle instabilities inherent in electronic components.

A second problem is that the two units must start at *exactly* the same time. If one starts as little as 15 milliseconds (1 millisecond equals $1/1000$th of a second) or so behind the other, you will hear an annoying "slapback echo" effect.

The solution to the first problem is to use the same master clock to provide a common timing reference to all devices in the system. However, each device must have certain hardware features in order for this concept to work:

1. *An external clock input (usually present as a rear panel jack).* The clock signal from the master can be patched into this jack, thus feeding timing pulses into the slave unit.
2. *A means to select between the external and internal clock,* since any slave devices must follow the external clock signal rather than their internal clocks. Usually a switch handles this function.
3. *The master device must have a clock output signal available at a jack.* This signal provides the timing reference for all the other elements in the system.

Now refer to **Fig. 1-7** to see how this all comes together. The master drum machine selects its internal clock and serves as the system's master clock; its clock output signal feeds the sequencer and a second drum machine. These latter two devices are switched to accept the external clock signal plugged into their external clock jacks. However, we still need a way to start all the devices at the same time. For this, each device needs a *start/stop* (also called *run/stop*) input. (Note: Some systems combine the clock and start/stop into a single signal; this gives less overall control than separate clock and start/stop signals.)

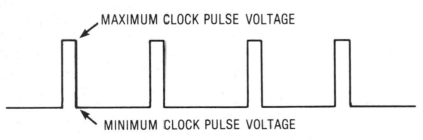

Figure 1-6

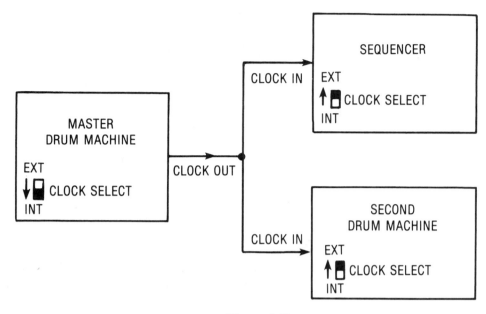

Figure 1-7

Starting and Stopping

When its power is first turned on, a drum machine (or sequencer, for that matter) is usually stopped, regardless of whether you have selected an internal or external clock. Most drums have a front panel start/stop switch: press it once and the drums start drumming; press again and the drums stop. Generally there is also a jack on the back that lets you control this function remotely via footswitch . . . press the footswitch once and the drums start, press again to stop. In the case of a master unit, starting the machine will often send the clock signal out the clock out jack.

Suppose next that each of the three units in **Fig. 1-7** includes a start/stop input. In most cases we can connect these all together and run them from a single footswitch, thus giving us the option to turn all the devices on simultaneously with one press of the foot-switch. As soon as the switch closes, the master starts sending out pulses and the slave devices start counting those pulses.

Great! We now have a situation where all machines start and stop at the same time and follow the same master timing reference, which means they are in sync with each other. So our problems are solved, right?

Well . . . not always, which brings us to the "different clock rate" problem.

Different Clock Rates

Since our tempo reference needs to be musically useful, we need to relate the number of pulses to beats and measures. Clock rates are specified in *pulses per quarter note* (ppqn). For example, suppose a sequencer that follows a 24 ppqn standard is set to receive an external clock; the sequencer counts the number of pulses it receives, and each pulse advances the sequence $1/24$th of a beat. Therefore, 24 pulses elapse for every beat, and consequently 96 pulses (4 times 24) would elapse during one measure (4 beats) of $4/4$ music. Unfortunately, though, different units have different clock rates. Common rates are 24 ppqn (used by Roland, E-mu, and Sequential), 48 ppqn (favored by Linn and older Korg gear), and 96 ppqn (the Oberheim standard). The Fairlight CMI requires a 384-ppqn clock; and older PPGs, 64 ppqn.

If an Oberheim device provides the master clock that feeds a Roland drum machine and Oberheim sequencer, you've got a problem: the sequencer will advance $1/96$th of a beat every time it counts a clock pulse, but the drum machine (which works on a 24-ppqn standard) will advance $1/24$th of a beat for each clock pulse received. Therefore, during the time it takes for the sequencer to play one beat (96 pulses), the drum machine will have played an entire measure.

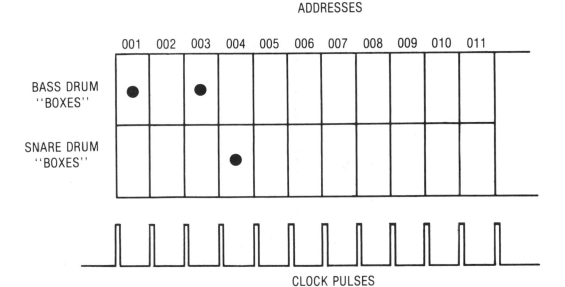

Figure 1-8

One solution employed by E-mu is to let the user divide the external clock frequency by any integer. Thus, if you're feeding the 24-ppqn Drumulator from a 96-ppqn Oberheim sequencer, you would simply divide the Oberheim master clock signal entering the Drumulator by a factor of 4 so that the Drumulator counts only every fourth pulse. This slows down the Drumulator so that, like the Oberheim, it advances one beat for every 96 pulses it receives.

Before going any further, let's explain why these particular numbers were chosen. The reason is that musical devices need to accommodate a variety of rhythmic values; the easiest way to get this point across is with some examples, but first we need to examine a bit about how drum machines store information.

A drum machine is basically a big memory bank composed of individual memory *addresses*. An analogy would be a big post office (the bank) composed of individual post office boxes (the addresses). When you start a drum machine, its clock steps through each address and looks to see whether any drums have been programmed to occur at that particular address. In **Fig. 1-8** the clock steps through the various addresses—we'll assume that each address represents one beat. Whenever the drum machine reads information from a particular address showing that a certain drum sound

was programmed to occur at that address, it sends out a trigger pulse to the appropriate drum sound generator. In our example, on the first clock pulse, which selects the first address, you would hear the bass drum. On the second clock pulse, you would hear nothing. On the third clock pulse, you would hear the bass drum again; and on the fourth clock pulse, you would hear the snare.

If we only needed to program drum sounds on every beat, a 1 ppqn system would work just fine. But in the example above, suppose we wanted to program a sound between the third and fourth clock pulses; it cannot be done. What we would have to do is double the number of addresses to accommodate this extra sound, as shown in **Fig. 1-9**. Every time we increase the number of clock pulses per quarter note, we increase the *resolution*—the ability of the drum machine to program "detailed" rhythms. Therefore, with a 1-ppqn system, the fastest note we can play is a quarter note. With a 2-ppqn system, we can program eighth (or slower) notes; with 4-ppqn system, sixteenth notes; and so on. Therefore, if we wanted to program thirty-second notes, an 8-ppqn system would do just fine since there are eight thirty-second notes to every quarter note. With an 8-ppqn system, every tick of the master clock represents a thirty-second note.

But there's something missing: What about triplets? Unfortunately, 8 ppqn is not

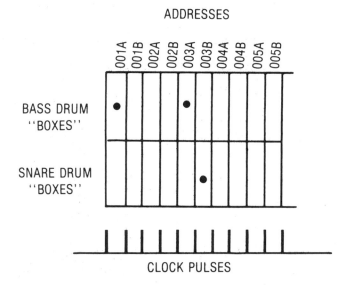

ADDRESSES

001A 001B 002A 002B 003A 003B 004A 004B 005A 005B

BASS DRUM "BOXES"

SNARE DRUM "BOXES"

CLOCK PULSES

THERE IS NOW AN ADDRESS BETWEEN THE THIRD AND FOURTH BEATS WHERE WE CAN PROGRAM A BEAT.

Figure 1-9

divisible by three. After a little bit of research, some companies figured 24 ppqn was the best way to go, as this accommodates up to thirty-second notes and thirty-second note triplets (see **Fig. 1-10**). As the figure shows, no matter where you want to program a sound—up to thirty-second note triplets—there will be a corresponding address into which it can be programmed. As the clock steps through the addresses, you will hear the various notes you programmed.

Now we're getting somewhere. But why do some manufacturers use 24 ppqn, some 48, some 96, and so on?

Well, as previously noted, the more pulses per quarter note, the greater the resolution. A system that uses 48 ppqn can provide sixty-fourth notes and sixty-fourth note triplets, which are not all that common but might be required from time to time. A 96-ppqn clock gives even better resolution. More resolution helps avoid the "robotic" feel of super-precise, auto-corrected timing; you can play beats that slightly lag or lead the tempo. High-resolution clocks also provide more realistic "doubling" effects, since the doubled part can be offset by very small time increments if desired. High resolution is also useful for film work (see sidebar). However, the higher the resolution, the higher the overall complexity—and therefore cost.

Fortunately, for most music 24 ppqn is perfectly adequate, so that has been adopted as the standard MIDI timing reference. Since all MIDI equipment counts at the same rate from a consistent clock signal, everything stays neatly in sync.

We still have one remaining problem with our clock pulse counting scheme (sorry). You'll recall that we need to start all our machines at the same time and have them start counting from a common point. Therefore, in order to sync multiple devices, they all must start from the beginning of a composition. But what if you want to start a song from, say, measure number 45? What's needed is some way to preset all units to measure number 45, then press the start/stop switch to have them start at the same time. Until MIDI, instruments did not have this capability; when you pressed **start**, they started from the beginning . . . period. Therefore, all units had to start at the beginning of a sequence to remain in sync.

MIDI solves this problem with an ingenious feature called a *song position pointer*, or simply, song pointer. Later on we'll cover this in more detail, but the basic idea is that MIDI keeps track of how many MIDI clock ticks have occurred since the beginning of a composition. For an example of how this is

High-Resolution Clocks in Film and Video

Sequencers are being used more and more in film and video work to trigger sound effects in time with visual cues occurring on-screen. High resolution is very important for this application: if a door slams and you hear the sound effect of a door slamming a fraction of a second later, the illusion is lost—the sound effect must occur within a few milliseconds of the visual cue.

With a 24-ppqn sequencer running at 120 beats per minute, a pulse suitable for triggering a sound effect occurs every 20.4 milliseconds. This does not offer sufficient resolution for many applications. But a 96-ppqn sequencer running at 120 beats per minute provides a pulse every 5.1 ms—much better. The fastest MIDI can send out a trigger pulse, under the best of conditions, is about 1/3 ms (the 320 microseconds it takes to send a MIDI clock message). SMPTE, a highly accurate synchronization protocol used extensively in the film and video industries, can provide resolution down to 0.4 ms. SMPTE will be covered later on in the book.

used, consider a sequencer/drum machine combination. If you want both units to start playing from measure number 20, no problem: Simply set the sequencer start point at measure 20, and the drum machine (which is slaved to the sequencer) will automatically set itself to the same place (measure 20). Tell them to start, and not only do they start together and count at the same rate, *they start from the same measure.* (Unfortunately, though, not all MIDI sequencers and drum machines include the song pointer feature.)

Pre-MIDI Synchronization Schemes

You might think it's not such a bright idea to discuss pre-MIDI devices in a MIDI world, but there are two reasons for this. One (as stated earlier) is that much of MIDI's original purpose was to solve problems inherent in older systems; and by understanding the older systems, we will have a firm foundation for understanding MIDI. The second is that many pre-MIDI devices are still in common

use, and knowing how they work will give us clues on how to synchronize them to MIDI devices.

The sync bus. In 1970 Charles Cohen (a member of an electronic music trio I formed called Anomali) devised a way for the band members to synchronize to each other. The idea was simple: run a sync cable between all the musicians, and let each musician have a switch that connected the cable to either the clock out, or external clock in, of his instrument. At any given moment, one member would switch to **clock out** and send a master clock signal out on to the sync bus. The others would then switch to **clock in** and be synchronized. As different tunes occurred, each musician would select whether they would provide the system clock or follow it.

Sync-to-tape. During the 70s many musicians discovered that they could record a clock signal on tape and use the taped signal as an external clock source. In most cases the signal coming off the tape was too low in level and not sufficiently "square," so this

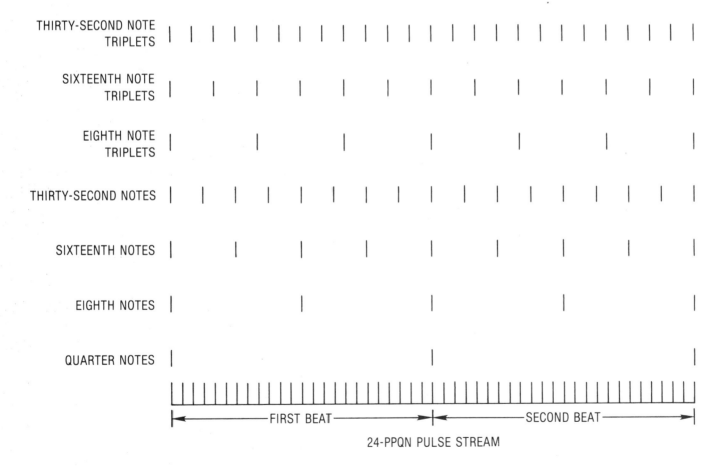

Figure 1–10

approach required some signal conditioning in order to turn the taped signal into a waveform suitable for use as a clock signal.

This was quite a breakthrough, because it meant that instruments could be synchronized during tape overdubs. Prior to sync-to-tape, if you wanted to record a drum machine part on tape it would be set to its internal clock and captured on tape as audio. Now suppose you wanted to do an overdub with that same drum machine. If the internal clock speed remained identical to when the part was recorded, and if you started the over-dubbed drum at exactly the same time as the previously recorded part, there was a slim possibility that the two would stay in sync long enough to record the overdub. However, if the tape speed varied even a little bit, or you nudged the tempo knob on the drum machine, that was that . . . end of overdub session. With sync-to-tape, the master clock could be preserved on tape. Even if you came back to do a drum overdub a few months later, your tempo reference would still be there.

Still, this system needed some improvements. For one thing, although you could drive drum machines and similar devices, there wasn't much else you could do with the taped tempo reference. For this reason I designed a box called the Master Synchronizer, which took a clock pulse recorded on tape and generated a number of timing signals from this main signal. In addition to conditioning the tape signal in order to provide a suitable clock signal to drum machines and the like, it also produced trigger pulses at a regular rate (every quarter note, eighth note, sixteenth note, triplets, etc.). These could drive synthesizer arpeggiators or trigger other events (play individual electronic drum sounds, switch effects on and off, etc.). With a Master Synchronizer, you not only had sync-to-tape but could also synchronize other events (like the synthesizer arpeggiators) to a master clock.

Although recording a clock signal on tape was better than nothing, problems remained. As mentioned earlier, with simple clock pulse systems all devices have to start from the same point (the beginning of the clock pulse generation), whereupon they all count together. This means that, when doing

sync-to-tape, if you wanted to overdub only the last two measures in a piece, you still had to rewind the tape all the way back to the beginning, sync the device being overdubbed to the sync track, and twiddle your thumbs until the last two measures, whereupon you could record the overdub. Another problem was that after shuttling tape around for a while occasionally some tape oxide would shed off and create a dropout, thereby eliminating a pulse or two from the click track. If you tried to overdub an instrument by following a messed up click track, it would be impossible to maintain sync with tracks which had been synched to the click track before the dropout occurred . . . so once there was a dropout, perfect sync would be lost forever.

Several manufacturers chose *FSK synchronization* as a more reliable sync-to-tape method. Instead of simply recording on/off clock pulses on tape, this sync system shifts between two different frequencies (hence the term *Frequency Shift Keying*). Tape is much happier recording alternating audio tones than clock pulses, and this system is also somewhat less sensitive to dropouts. As a result, many manufacturers started to use FSK sync-to-tape systems.

Unfortunately, each manufacturer chose their own standard. So, if you put a Linn sync track down on tape, you could not sync a Roland or Oberheim drum unit to that same track. However, since many units had external clock outputs and inputs, you could do some roundabout tricks. For example, a drum unit could sync to the FSK track, then its clock output could drive another unit's clock input (see **Fig. 1-11**). Still, you could run into the problem where one unit required a clock rate different from another. If you tried to sync a 96-ppqn Oberheim drum unit to a 48-ppqn Linn, the Oberheim would run at half-speed compared to the Linn. Of course, you could always program the Oberheim in double time, but this starts to get pretty complicated.

When enough musicians get frustrated, someone else sees a product. About the same time I designed the Master Synchronizer for budget sync applications, Garfield Electronics introduced the Doctor Click for high-end sync applications. This was intended to be a

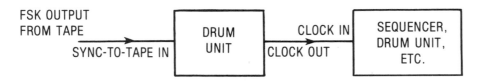

Figure 1–11

universal clock transmitter/receiver/translator, and it did a very good job. You could take just about any sync track recorded on tape and translate it to just about any other format. If you needed to sync Roland to Oberheim, Korg to E-mu, or Linn to Sequential Circuits, no problem. You could even take a *click track* (metronome signal recorded on tape) and synthesize a sync track at the proper rate—24, 48, or 96 ppqn. Garfield subsequently introduced several lower-cost units designed to solve other, more specific problems.

Although problem-solver boxes such as the Doctor Click were very useful, they were still band-aid solutions: The underlying problem, lack of standards and lack of design compatibility, remained . . . thus giving further impetus to MIDI's creation.

Probably the closest thing to MIDI that existed prior to adoption of the MIDI standard was the Oberheim System. This comprised a drum unit, sequencer, and polyphonic keyboard that had all been designed specifically to work with each other. You didn't have to worry about incompatible clock rates or other problems, unless you wanted to interface the System to non-Oberheim products. Actually, many of the System's attributes anticipated MIDI; for example, the sequencer could change synthesizer patches automatically. A couple of hit singles were written by System owners, who would work out parts at home then bring the System into the studio and just press **start**, whereupon the System would faithfully play back whatever sequences and rhythms had been programmed into the various devices.

The next major step after the System was the introduction of MIDI (incidentally, Oberheim eventually made a retrofit available for the System to make it MIDI-compatible). And you thought we were never going to get around to MIDI! Well read on, because now we're finally ready for the Big Wrap-Up

. . . it's time to check out some MIDI basics, then to see how MIDI solves the problems we've mentioned in this chapter.

MIDI BASICS

Now that we've discussed some of the problems involved with electronic music instruments, and early solutions, let's investigate how MIDI solves those problems. First, though, we need to know a bit more about what makes MIDI tick.

The MIDI Cord

An instrument already has an AC cord that carries electrical power, and an audio cord that carries audio signals to an amplifier. Now we have a third cord: the MIDI cable. This carries neither audio nor power but instead transmits *information* (data) about the status of the instrument to, and receives "status reports" from, other MIDI instruments. This information is coded in a computer language . . . a somewhat primitive language with few words and several dialects, but a language nonetheless.

Chapter 4 describes this language in detail, but let's give a quick overview right now.

The most basic type of information the MIDI language conveys concerns *notes*—which notes are being played and for how long. MIDI also transmits *timing and synchronization data* so that drum machines, sequencers, and keyboards can all start, stop, and play together. *Program changes* are also part of the information package, so that if you select, say, a particular program on one synthesizer, any slave synthesizers will change programs as well so that their sounds can complement the sounds coming from the master synth.

The *song pointer* is another very useful piece of MIDI information; as mentioned earlier, it keeps track of where you are in a composition.

Now that we know a little bit about the kind of information we're going to transmit and receive, we need a way to physically carry this information from one MIDI device to another. A MIDI cord (see **Fig. 1-12**) has two connectors joined by a length of cable less than 50 feet long. The reason for not exceeding a particular length is to avoid degrading the quality of the signal passing through the cable. Generally, the shorter a MIDI cable you can use in a particular situation, the better.

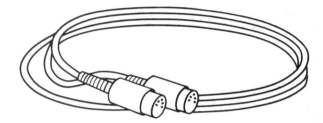

Figure 1-12. *MIDI cord*

The connectors are typically five-pin DIN connectors (see **Fig. 1-13**). DIN connectors have been used in Europe for many years and are starting to catch on in this country as well. At present the MIDI signal requires only three of the five terminals for operation, although there is speculation that the other two terminals will be used someday as MIDI evolves.

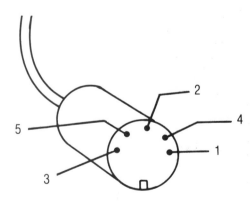

FRONT VIEW
MALE DIN CONNECTOR PIN NUMBERING

Figure 1-13. *DIN connectors*

DIN connectors are commonly available and inexpensive, but they are also not particularly durable. As a result, some manufacturers use three-conductor XLR connectors

(see **Fig. 1-14**) for their MIDI cables. According to the original MIDI spec (see Appendix A), using XLR connectors is allowable providing that the manufacturer furnish appropriate adapters to fit DIN-type equipment.

It is very important to use a quality cord designed for MIDI applications. Information is transmitted along this cord at a very high rate of speed, so it is not wise to use a cord designed for "normal" audio applications. A proper MIDI cable will also shield against possible interference from other electrical devices operating in the same vicinity.

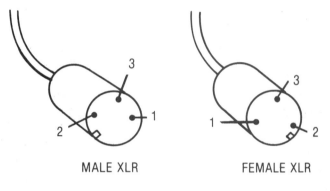

MALE XLR   FEMALE XLR

FRONT VIEW
XLR CONNECTOR PIN NUMBERING

Figure 1-14. *XLR connectors*

MIDI Jacks

There are three types of MIDI jacks: MIDI In, MIDI Out, and MIDI Thru. Simply stated, the MIDI Out jack transmits data, and the MIDI In jack receives data (just like an audio output jack sends out audio, and an audio input jack receives audio). For example, if a master keyboard is controlling a slave keyboard, the MIDI Out from the master would connect to the MIDI In of the slave. As the master transmits information (such as which notes are being played), the slave receives this information and does whatever the master says. If the master says, **note middle C on**, the slave will start playing middle C until another MIDI command tells it to turn the note off. See **Fig. 1-15**.

Most instruments have both MIDI Out and MIDI In connectors so that they may transmit and receive data, depending on what is required for a particular application. The

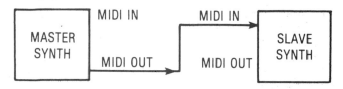

Figure 1-15

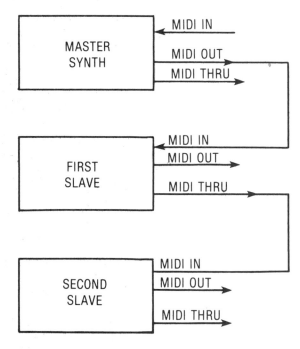

Figure 1-17

MIDI Thru jack is something else altogether; it carries a *replica* of the signal appearing at the MIDI In jack. MIDI Thru is like having a built-in MIDI *Y-cord* (see **Fig. 1-16**) that allows several slaves to be connected to the same master. Thru jacks should be used carefully, as we'll discuss later.

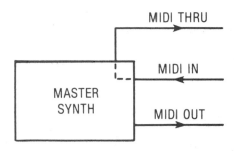

THE MIDI THRU SIGNAL IS A REPLICA OF THE MIDI IN SIGNAL ENTERING THE MASTER SYNTH.

Figure 1-16

WHAT IS MIDI GOOD FOR?

Let's close this chapter by describing some of the ways that MIDI can help you both live and in the studio. All of the following will be described in greater detail later on in the book.

Bigger sound. As noted before, a MIDI master can control a slave synthesizer by connecting the master's MIDI Out to the slave's MIDI In, thus providing "doubling" or "layering" effects. However, for an even thicker sound the MIDI Thru on the slave can connect to the MIDI In on a second slave, which gives "tripling" effects (see **Fig. 1-17**).

Reducing equipment clutter. One of the main advantages of MIDI is that a single "mother" keyboard controller can play multiple "offspring" synthesizers, which might well be hidden offstage. This single controller could be a lightweight, easy-to-maneuver portable keyboard or a deluxe quality, piano-action keyboard. Most mother keyboards also include switches, modulation wheels, and other devices designed to access other MIDI

parameters (for example, virtually all mother keyboards have **program select** switches for remotely selecting different programs on the slaves).

The slave keyboards can be standard synthesizers or small expander boxes that have no keyboard but are instead MIDI-controlled sound generators (after all, if you're feeding these instruments from a remote keyboard, why bother to have a keyboard on the slave synthesizer at all).

New controllers. Anything that transmits MIDI signals can control MIDI expander boxes, sequencers, and the like (just as any guitar with an output jack can feed any amplifier). Although keyboards were the first MIDI controllers, there are now guitar controllers that produce MIDI, and even devices that derive MIDI information from single-note melody lines (such as those produced by flutes, saxophones, the human voice, etc.). Electric drum units also provide MIDI outputs, which can trigger other MIDI-compatible drums, expander boxes, or synthesizers.

Computer control. MIDI allows for simple home computers to talk to musical instruments, which has many implications. As mentioned, through MIDI we can change programs on a synthesizer; imagine that we have several synthesizers hooked up to a computer and the computer issues a **program change** command when required—even in the middle of a song—so you don't have to lift your fingers off the keys. And speaking of live performance, some signal processors (digital delays, digital reverbs, mixers, and even lighting controllers) now include MIDI inputs and react to program changes; thus, special effects can be easily coordinated with music.

The tapeless studio and the MIDI back-up band. These are two of my favorite applications. You can partition a computer's memory into different tracks, just like a tape recorder, and record note information for different instruments in different tracks of computer memory. On playback each track can drive its own instrument, thus allowing you to sequence several instruments simultaneously. Because the note data is in memory, it can be easily modified and edited. And if you're a singer, this same principle can be used to program your own back-up band! MIDI computer/sequencers are very powerful devices, and we'll spend a lot of time on the subject in Chapter 7.

Improving your music theory chops. Because instruments can be hooked up to computers, it's easy to write programs that, for example, show the notes you are playing on the lines of staff. Other MIDI computer programs let you print out compositions in standard notation.

End of many standardization problems. MIDI means that you no longer have to worry about control voltage and gate compatibility, since the MIDI specification is unambiguous about such things as what "word" corresponds to what note. Also, because MIDI provides for timing and synchronization, all MIDI equipment synchronizes together without your having to think about clock pulse rates, signal levels, and so on. This is the kind of thing that MIDI does best—take over housekeeping chores so that you can be creative. While there are different MIDI "dialects" used by different manufacturers, the commonalities far outweigh any differences.

MIDI also provides a common language for older equipment. Roland makes converters for most of its equipment so that they can talk MIDI. It's even possible to control a vintage 1970 minimoog via MIDI if you have the right converter box (which we'll cover towards the end of the book in the chapter on accessories).

Less obsolescence and greater cost-effectiveness. Once you buy your MIDI mother keyboard, you can expand the system easily with additional expander modules and MIDI gear—it is no longer necessary for every synthesizer to have a keyboard. This also means that you can really "learn" a particular keyboard rather than having to jump around from synthesizer to synthesizer. And when it's time to sell a MIDI keyboard, it should hold its resale value reasonably well providing it can work with newer, more sophisticated MIDI equipment.

Since many MIDI instruments are software-based (and if you don't know what that means, you will by the end of next chapter!), updates and modifications are much more feasible than with hardware-based instruments. The net result is that for the cost of a single chip change you can often add a whole bunch of new features to a particular piece of equipment.

Yes, MIDI is lots of fun. But to really understand how it works, and therefore make the most of its potential, you need to get "under the hood" of your instrument. What you'll find is a . . . computer! Don't panic, though. We don't need to become programmers, or get out a soldering iron, or anything like that. Actually, the computers used in MIDI equipment are pretty simple, quite friendly, and extremely reliable. Once you have an idea of how computers work, even if it's solely from a conceptual standpoint, you will have found the essence of MIDI. The concepts of information, data, memory, programs, software, and all of that unintelligible stuff will suddenly fall into place and you'll see MIDI as the *musically-oriented communications network* that it really is.

There's a bit of a challenge coming up, but the rewards are worth it. Without further ado, let's meet the computer inside your musical instrument.

Chapter 2

The Computer/ Instrument Connection

What's a Computer Doing in My Instrument?

Computers like to work with numbers, and music can be expressed mathematically. Not surprisingly, computers and musical instruments get along very well together.

There's a computer in your drum machine, in your polyphonic synthesizer, maybe even in your effects programmer. How did computers— devices that used to cost zillions of bucks and take up an entire room—end up inside your musical instrument?

Actually, it was a case of good fortune. Just when musical instruments really needed computers, the Silicon Valley technoids put computers on little chips for little bucks; and the rest is history.

Programmable synthesizers were the first mass-market musical instruments to include computers. At first, the computers just remembered knob settings and other patch information. Next, they started doing spiffy arpeggiation tricks. Then companies started replacing traditional analog circuitry with computerized equivalents (for example, the computer was often put to use generating envelopes and LFO modulation waveforms).

The computer takeover didn't stop there. Most synthesizers include accessories once considered the domain of Serious Computers, such as tape interfaces and disk drives . . . and now the instrument's computers are being put to use handling MIDI and providing on-board sequencing. Computers are important in today's music, so let's get down and digital.

How a Computer Massages Data

We're going to be talking about *data* throughout the book, so let's define our terms before going any further. Data is just a shorthand word for *information,* usually expressed in the form of numbers. MIDI data is often about notes—what pitch they are, how loud they are, and when they should start and stop playing. Computers, however, don't care what the data is about: it's all just numbers to them. This chapter covers basic stuff about how computers work with data, so that *you* can work easily with the computers on which MIDI depends.

Let's begin by considering a very sophisticated computer system—you. You contain many of the same elements as a computer, which makes coming up with an analogy pretty simple.

A simple *program* that you might *run* on your human computer (the brain) would be playing a piano as you read from sheet music. To an accomplished musician, this process is so automatic as to be second-nature—but at some point, that musician was a struggling student having to examine each task step-by-step. A computer works in much the same way: It is taught how to do a task step-by-step, then executes these steps at a very high rate of speed.

You make a computer do something step-by-step by giving it a sequence of *instructions,* with each instruction describing one step. This sequence of instructions is called a *program.*

If you were to be "programmed" to read sheet music, your list of instructions might go something like this:

1. Sit down at the piano and get comfortable.
2. Set up the sheet music.
3. Read ("input") several pieces of "data" (information): the time signature, tempo, and key.
4. Scan the page with your eyes until you find the first note to play.

5. Input the note into your brain and remember it temporarily.

6. Check your memory for the note symbols you learned as a student. Then compare the note input in step 5 with these symbols to properly identify the note.

7. Upon identifying the note, decide which finger of which hand should play the note.

8. "Output" a nerve impulse down your arm to move your finger.

9. Scan the page with your eyes until you find the next note to play.

10. If there is another note, return to step 5. Otherwise, proceed to the next step.

11. End.

If that made sense to you, congratulations . . . you now know the basics of how computers work. All that remains is to relate the above concepts to the hardware actually used in a computer, and you'll be well on your way.

There are several important elements in the example of the the piano player: First, there is the program itself. While shown above as a list of instructions, in reality your "piano-playing program" is stored permanently in your memory as part of the process of learning the piano. In fact, you could call practicing the piano programming your brain to play the piano.

Then we have *input devices*, such as the eyes and ears. The eyes form an *interface* (go-between) between the printed page and your brain, while your ears listen to the results of your playing and confirm that you played the desired notes. (You can also think of the ears as *error-correction* devices since they detect if a mistake has been made, whereupon your brain will usually direct your fingers to try playing the note again.)

The *output devices* would be your arms, hands, and feet (the latter for the pedals, unless you're Jerry Lee Lewis).

Note that we are actually using two different types of memory while playing the piano. As mentioned above, there is the permanent memory that stores the program. The other type is more of a "scratchpad" memory that holds the notes you read long enough for you to play them, then forgets about those notes and moves on to the next batch of notes. In a computer the permanent type of memory that holds many of the machine's programs is called *ROM* (short for Read-Only Memory). The temporary type is called *RAM* (for Random-Access Memory, which loosely translated means that you can alter it easily—unlike ROM, which is "etched in stone"). With home computers ROM-based programs usually come in cartridge form; these are very hard to update. These days, computers usually read programs into RAM from a disk, so that programs can be easily updated by using a new or updated disk.

And what processes all this input and output, compares new data to data stored in memory, and generally keeps track of things? In a computer it's called the *processor*, which is the equivalent of the part of your brain that reasons and makes decisions.

Elements of a Computer

The human computer is a marvelous, remarkable feat of engineering; the ones we build are pretty puny by comparison—they're slower, less efficient, harder to program, and don't go to parties or listen to music. But they're good enough for our purposes.

The processor (also called the CPU or Central Processing Unit) provides the computer's intelligence. The CPU accepts input data from the input devices, makes decisions based on this data, sends data to memory, pulls data from memory, sends data to output devices, and generally is the boss of the organization. With a computer-controlled synthesizer, playing a note on the keyboard sends data describing that note to the processor. The processor then decides what to do with the data, based on how it is *programmed*. As with the program for humans given earlier, the computer's program consists of a series of logical steps that instruct the computer how to do a task. Here's a greatly simplified version of a program that would scan the keyboard and send **note on** and **note off** information through the MIDI connector:

1. Scan the keyboard to see which, if any, keys are down.

2. If a new key is down, skip to step 4.

3. If no key is down, return to step 1.

4. Send the appropriate **note on** data to the MIDI connector.

5. Check to see if any keys have been released.

6. If a key has been released, skip to step 8.

7. If a key has not been released, return to step 1.
8. Send the appropriate **note off** data to the MIDI connector.
9. Return to step 1.

It's worth studying this program in some depth, since it will give you a feel for how computers think. Step 3 is important, since it makes sure that the program will always "loop" back to the beginning until it finds that a key(s) is down. Only then does it follow the instructions in step 2 and proceed with the rest of the program. Step 6 deals with the **note off** information, while step 7 jumps back to the beginning to check whether additional notes are down. If the computer has had to send **note off** data (step 8), it will move on to step 9 after sending the data; this step sends the computer back to step 1, and the process starts all over again.

However, be aware that the actual program for scanning a keyboard is far more complex. Each step above represents many more detailed steps. For example, step 1 might actually consist of a separate command to check each key (check whether low C is down, check whether the key above low C is down, check whether the key two steps above low C is down, and so forth until it has checked the entire keyboard).

Also remember that all this happens at extremely high rates of speed—the entire keyboard scan will usually take less than a millisecond ($1/1000$th of a second; see sidebar). During that time the computer will have executed many instructions just to do that one keyboard scan. The main reason why computers are so useful is that they can do repetitive tasks very rapidly.

Computer Memory

But there's more to life than scanning keyboards . . . at some point the processor might want to store (remember) data for later use. As one example, a simple *arpeggiation* program might scan which keys are down but, instead of playing them all at once, play them sequentially starting with the lowest note and ending with the highest note. However, some synthesizers with an arpeggiation "latch" feature can store the note data in memory so that even if you lift your fingers off the keys, the arpeggio will continue playing. This is one simple application of memory.

Scanning Delays

Some keyboard players can notice slight timing errors when they play a computer-controlled keyboard; in other words, the timing just isn't as "tight" as they would like. But as mentioned in the body of the text, the entire scan takes less than a millisecond . . . so what's the problem?

Delays can occur because of what the computer does *between* scans. During this time it is monitoring the MIDI data, perhaps calculating envelope shapes, sending messages to a display, and so on. As a result, successive scans may be separated by as much as 15 milliseconds. Most instruments seem to do a scan around every 10 ms or so, which is not an objectionable delay by any means.

Note that this arpeggiation program arpeggiates the notes upwards. We could rewrite the program so that it would again play the keys sequentially but this time start with the highest note and end with the lowest note to produce a downward arpeggio. We could have the arpeggiation occur randomly, or scan up and down, or play notes in the order in which they were played on the keyboard, whatever—all it takes is a program change (i.e., a different set of instructions). We could even make the program scan an arpeggiator "mode" switch. With the **up** mode selected, the computer would jump to a part of the program that caused notes to arpeggiate upwards; with the **down** mode selected, the computer would jump to a part of the program that caused notes to arpeggiate downwards.

Before moving on to the next subject, we should note that all of the pseudo-programs we've mentioned have been written in English instead of computer talk. The actual language a computer uses is numbers; each instruction the computer can execute (such as **load a piece of data into the memory, fetch a value from the memory, add two numbers together,** and the like) is coded with a unique numerical value. Therefore, a program—which consists of a set of instructions—is, in its most basic form, really just a series of numbers. When you first turn on the computer, it does whatever it's told to do by the first instruction of the program, then moves on from there until the program is complete (or you turn off the power).

Now let's look at how a computer receives its input and how it sends its output, and that will pretty much take care of the introduction.

I/O and the Data Buss

Our five (optionally six) senses are fantastic interface devices. The ears can resolve air pressure changes over a 1,000,000,000,000:1 range, and our eyes can cover a little over an octave of the visual spectrum. Computers do not have these wonderful transducers. Instead, they rely on switches being closed and opened, controls being turned, and voltages being translated into data the computer can understand. The input and output devices hooked to a computer are referred to as I/O (pronounced eye-oh) devices.

One limitation is that a computer can only make yes/no, on/off decisions; it does not know the meaning of "maybe." Therefore, if you're trying to measure a voltage, the computer will figure out the value by asking a series of questions: is the voltage greater than 1 volt? greater than 2 volts? less than 3 volts? and so on until it zeroes in on the approximate value. The reason why I say approximate is that this yes/no process can resolve only a certain range of numbers (once you start asking questions like, is the voltage greater than 1.000000000001 volts? less than 1.000000000002 volts? you're really splitting hairs). The reason for this lack of resolution is a little too complex to go into just now, but suffice it to say that computers prefer simple, unambiguous input data that can be understood without having to ask lots of questions. Switches are a great way to communicate with a computer because of their unambiguity—they are either on or off.

A potentiometer (a "pot") is more difficult to "read" because an analog pot is continuously variable and in theory covers an infinite number of points along its travel. A computer cannot deal with concepts like infinity (hey, it's hard enough for humans), so it divides up the control into steps—maybe 128, or 256, or 512 little steps. **Fig. 2-1** shows a potentiometer that is *quantized* into 8 steps. Depending upon where the knob is pointing, the computer will read either 1, 2, 3, 4, 5, 6, 7, or 8 as the value of the potentiometer. Even if the pot moves around within one of the quantized zones, the computer will read the same value (**Fig. 2-2**).

A POTENTIOMETER QUANTIZED INTO EIGHT STEPS

Figure 2-1

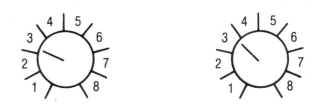

IN BOTH CASES, THE COMPUTER READS THE POT'S VALUE AS "3."

Figure 2-2

But what, you might ask, occurs if the knob is pointing right on the line between the two zones? This can sometimes produce "jitter" where the computer has a hard time deciding exactly which zone it is reading. The result is an unstable reading, but with most hardware you will not encounter this problem. (Knobs are usually quantized in more than eight steps; we just used eight for the sake of keeping the illustration simple.)

Once the data is in a form the computer can read, we send it along on the *data buss*. The data buss is like the computer's central nervous system: it conveys electrical impulses from the input devices to the CPU and from the CPU to the output devices.

As an example of how the data buss works, suppose we have a programmable synthesizer that stores 10 control settings in memory. A program to do this task might look something like . . . .

1. Read control 1, and put its value on the data buss so that the CPU can read it.
2. Have the CPU read the value on the data buss.
3. Have the CPU send the value to memory location 1.

4. Have the CPU read control 2, and put its value on the data buss so that the CPU can read it.
5. Have the CPU read the value on the data buss.
6. Have the CPU send the value to memory location 2.

. . . and so on, until all 10 control values have been read and stored in memory. The last step would be, return to step 1, so that the controls would be repetitively scanned and stored in memory. Thus, if you change a knob the CPU will send this new data to memory and update the previously stored setting.

Addressing

But how does the computer know which control it is reading out of the many possible controls? It does this by assigning each control a unique *address*. If the computer asks for the reading from the control at address 7, only that control's reading will be placed on the data buss. The other controls will still be functioning, but the computer will not be reading them. When it wants to read control 8, the computer sends out the address corresponding to control 8. This is sort of like selecting one channel out of many on a TV set.

Memory locations also have addresses. In fact, it seems that just about everything in a computer has an address—it's not unlike some huge post office that has millions of little post office boxes, each with its own number. Want to know what's in memory address 451,632? Just look at the memory contents at that particular address.

What does all this mean? Not too much if you're only going to be playing with MIDI, since these little details are handled by the computer (after all, the value of computers is that they deal with trivia you don't want to have to think about). However, I'm touching briefly on these subjects for the sake of completeness and because musicians tend to be naturally curious types who like to know how things work.

The Numerical Nature of Music

Pitch can be expressed as a number (for example, A 440 Hz). So can tempo, such as 125 beats per minute. The resonant frequency of a filter, the rate of vibrato, the attack time of an envelope—all of these parameters can be expressed numerically. There are even ways to measure the loudness of a sound, in decibels (dB). Therefore, quantifying a synthesizer's sound solely by numbers is not only possible but can even give a reasonably accurate description of that sound. If I said that a synthesizer is playing an A 110 Hz, with a filter frequency cutoff of 220 Hz, and I was adding 10 percent vibrato at 4 Hz, *providing that you knew the definitions of the terms*, you would know that I was talking about a fairly muted sound in the bass range with a little bit of slow vibrato.

This is the core of MIDI: the concept that music can be expressed numerically.

Because of this fact, computers can get involved—which means rapid data transfer and processing (remember our definition of data as "information expressed as numbers"). It also means that numbers representing musical notes can be shuttled from instrument to instrument and correctly interpreted. It means that we can have cheap sequencers that run on cheap computers yet produce expensive sounds, and it implies a whole lot more. All of this is possible because we now have a defined language for musical parameters. The invention of notation made it easier for musicians to share their work, but MIDI makes it possible to share *the actual fabric of the music itself*.

We're on the verge of unravelling the computer/synthesizer connection, so stay with me . . . we're almost there.

How a Computer Transmits and Receives Data

Like human languages a computer's language also involves "letters" and "words." Unlike English, though, the words represent numbers (not concepts) and there are only two letters: the numbers 1 and 0. The question now becomes how many numbers can you get out of 1 and 0, so let's get acquainted with the *binary number system*.

Yes, I know you didn't buy this book to become a mathematician . . . but having this background will come in handy when you eventually get more involved with MIDI's intricacies. Besides, what we're learning here applies to computers in general, not just MIDI; so you'll be that much better equipped to deal with these wonderful devices.

In the decimal numbering system, we have 10 available digits (0 through 9), probably because people counted on their fingers and toes back when numbers were being invented. Numbers greater than 9 can be expressed by adding a "tens" column to the left of the "units" column, and numbers greater than 99 can be expressed by adding a "hundreds" column to the left of the tens column.

Basically, we add up all the digits in the column to produce a total. For example, the number 579 really means $(5 \times 100) + (7 \times 10) + (9 \times 1)$, which of course equals 579. Like the piano player we mentioned earlier, we are so used to this numbering system we don't have to go through any mental calculations; we take in the number 579 all at once.

The binary numbering system has two available digits (0 and 1), because computers can only deal with on/off or yes/no. Counting to one is simple: 0, 1. Now how do we count to two? We'll take a cue from the decimal way of doing things and add another column to the left of the units column. Remember, though, in decimal the value of each number in a column is ten times the value of a number in the column immediately to the right. However, since we're dealing in binary (twos) rather than decimal (tens), the value of each number in a column is *two* times the value of the number in the column immediately to the right. Therefore, the column to the left of the ones column would be the twos column, the column to the left of the twos column would be the fours column, and so on as indicated in the example below.

Sixteens	Eights	Fours	Twos	Units
1	0	0	1	1

This is binary number 10011. Hmmmm . . . sure looks strange! But it can be analyzed very easily in the same way we analyzed the number 579 above. Namely, 10011 breaks down as

$$(1 \times 16) + (0 \times 8) + (0 \times 4) + (1 \times 2) + (1 \times 1)$$

which simplifies to

$$16 + 0 + 0 + 2 + 1 = 19.$$

Therefore, binary 10011 equals decimal 19.

Now don't panic!! You will not, repeat, will not need to translate numbers from binary to decimal in the process of using MIDI. You do not need to memorize binary values, and there will be no surprise quizzes. All that we're trying to get across is that

1. There is more than one way to count.
2. Computers count in twos rather than tens because it makes life easier for them.

Each digit in a binary word is called a *bit*, which can be either 1 or 0. A group of eight bits is called a *byte*. The highest number we can express with eight bits is 11111111. And if we figure that out it becomes . . .

$$(1 \times 128) + (1 \times 64) + (1 \times 32) + (1 \times 16) + (1 \times 8) + (1 \times 4) + (1 \times 2) + (1 \times 1)$$

which totals up to 255. The lowest number we can express is 00000000, so with an eight "word" (byte) we can express 256 unique numbers, from 0 to 255.

Of course, the more bits, the more numbers we can express (for example, a 16-bit word can express over 65,000 different numbers).

So what does all this mean to musicians? Well, these numbers are the nuts and bolts of the information transmitted by MIDI. Suppose a synthesizer's vibrato wheel is quantized to 128 steps (remember how we talked earlier of quantizing a pot to a certain number of steps?) and that we want to express its current position. Simple computers like to work with bytes (eight-bit words), and luckily 128 steps (0 through 127) can be expressed by using seven of the byte's eight bits. So, with the vibrato all the way off, the synthesizer would transmit the vibrato value as 00000000. With the vibrato wheel all the way up, the synth would transmit a vibrato value of 01111111 (127 decimal). In between the two extremes, it would transmit a value of 01000000 (64 decimal). (Incidentally, MIDI uses only seven bits of an eight-bit word to express a particular value; as we'll see later on, the eighth bit indicates the *type* of word.)

Parallel vs. Serial Transmission

There are two main methods used for transmitting bytes from one device to another. One is called *parallel transmission*, where all eight bits of a byte are sent at once from one machine to another (see **Fig. 2-3**). A good analogy would be speaking to a friend, where individual letters are grouped into words. For example, if you say "hi - how - are - you," it takes four events (words) to get the meaning across even though the message comprises many individual letters. Parallel transmission, while fast, requires multi-conductor cords and is somewhat more expensive to implement than *serial transmission*, the mode adopted for the MIDI specification.

With serial transmission, bits are sent *consecutively* (serially) along a single line (see **Fig. 2-4**). A good analogy would be saying one letter at a time; with serial transmission the message given above would be sent as "h-i (space) h-o-w (space) a-r-e (space) y-o-u." Note that, since each letter is sent separately, this method of transmission requires more events to get the meaning across. Also note that spaces must be inserted between each word so that the computer doesn't get confused as to where each word begins and ends.

Although serial transmission takes more time than parallel transmission, it is affordable and fast enough for all but the most intense applications. In fact, MIDI uses about a 50 percent faster data transfer rate than the computer industry's standard data transfer rate (see sidebar).

To wrap all this up, the essence of a MIDI transmission is packets of information (messages), sent one bit at a time, from one machine to another.

How MIDI Groups Words

The tide is turning from theory to practice . . . if you've followed along so far, you're almost out of the woods.

MIDI groups information in multibyte "sentences" or "messages" of one or more words. There are two types of MIDI words: *status* words (which identify a particular *function*, such as **note on**, **note off**, **pitch wheel change**, etc.) and *data* words (which give data on the function identified by the status word, such as which note is on and how much the pitch wheel has changed). With MIDI, status bytes always start with a 1 (such as 10000000) and data bytes with a 0 (such as 00000000) so that the computer can easily recognize how the data should be interpreted. As an example, let's look at the MIDI message for a **note on** event.

The complete **note on** event message comprises *three* eight-bit bytes (i.e., 10010000, 00001010, and 00010010). The first word (byte) is the status byte; the *first four bits* of the status byte identify the *function*, while the *second four bits* specify the *MIDI channel*. (The concept of

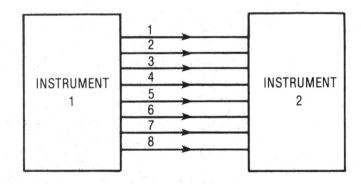

EACH LINE SENDS ONE BIT THUS TRANSFERRING EIGHT BITS (ONE BYTE) SIMULTANEOUSLY.

Figure 2–3

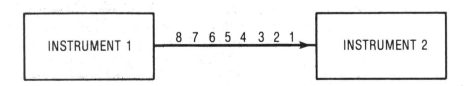

EIGHT BITS ARE SENT ONE AT A TIME OVER A SINGLE LINE.

Figure 2–4

Why Send Data Serially?

When MIDI was in its infancy, there was much debate over whether to adopt parallel transmission, which is far faster than serial transmission. However, parallel transmission requires more interconnecting wires between instruments, which leads to much more expensive connectors and can also create ground loop and hum problems. Using parallel transmission would have priced MIDI out of the market for low-cost gear, thus defeating the whole purpose of MIDI as a "universal language." Another reason is that the computers inside most instruments are incapable of handling superfast data rates anyway; they are pretty preoccupied with scanning keyboards, generating envelopes, running displays, and so on.

MIDI can transmit a new bit every 32 millionths of a second. It takes 8 bits to form a byte (the smallest usable unit of information) and another 2 bits to indicate the spaces between bytes, for a total of 10 bits per MIDI word. Each word therefore takes 320 millionths of a second to transmit, and over 3,000 MIDI words can be sent every second.

For comparison, the computer industry's standard serial data rates are 300 Baud (30 ten-bit characters per second, or 100 times slower than MIDI) and 1200 Baud (120 characters per second, or 25 times slower than MIDI). Even the fastest serial rate, 19,200 Baud, is still about a third slower than MIDI. Computers also require the equivalent of a MIDI word just to transmit a single character of text, which means that MIDI packs information more "densely" than standard computers.

While some would like to see an even higher data transmission rate for MIDI, universal acceptance of this kind of "hot rod" specification is realistically several years off. Besides, MIDI is fast enough for most musical applications and is inexpensive enough to be designed into virtually any electronic music instrument. The few cases where it isn't fast enough can often be handled by parceling out data between several independent MIDI lines or using special high-speed interfaces (such as RS-422) when you need to move huge amounts of data around quickly (such as digitized audio samples).

a MIDI channel will be explained in great detail in Chapter 3; don't worry too much about this for now, other than to know that MIDI can transmit information over 16 different channels.)

If the status byte's first four bits are 1001, that means a note has been played (**note on**) and that more information will be forthcoming about the note. The status byte's first four bits can indicate other functions as well: 1000 indicates that a note has been released; 1010 indicates that the data bytes indicate key pressure data; 1110 means that the data bytes contain pitch bend information; and so on. As noted earlier, these status bytes all start with 1. As soon as the computer receives a byte that starts with a 1, it knows it is receiving a status byte.

The next four bits of the **note on** event message specify the channel number over which the **note on** data is being sent, with 0000 being the lowest channel number and 1111 being the highest. However, here we run into a fine point. Since the concept of a channel 0 might confuse people, MIDI numbers them from 1 to 16 even though the binary channel numbers go from 0 to 15. Therefore, if you select channel 1 on an instrument, as far as the computer is concerned you are really selecting binary number 0000. If you select channel 2, you are really selecting binary number 0001. No big deal, but this could cause confusion later so I thought I'd mention it now.

Now that we've examined the status byte that starts the message, let's look at the data bytes that make up the rest of the message. As with the status byte, the first data byte is again eight bits long but starts with a 0, which leaves seven remaining bits for carrying other information. In the case of a **note on** event, these seven bits (which represent 128 different numbers) indicate the key number of the **note on** event. MIDI numbers each key of a keyboard, with middle C equal to 0111100 (60 in decimal). Typically, a five-octave keyboard ranges from 36 to 96, and an 88-note piano keyboard from 21 to 108 . . . so 128 notes cover a lot of territory.

The second and final data byte of the **note on** event also begins with 0. The remaining seven bits express the key velocity (i.e., how fast the key goes from up to down, which corresponds to how hard you hit the keys; this is useful for controlling dynamics) as a number from 0 to 127 (binary 0000000 to 1111111). If the keyboard doesn't have velocity control, MIDI sends out a default value of 64 (binary 1000000). Now let's summarize what we've learned by pressing middle C on a nonvelocity MIDI keyboard and sending it out over channel

1. Here's the information packet that comes out of the MIDI port:

10010000	0111100	01000000
status	data	data

Just to make sure we've got this under control, let's review. The first bit of any byte indicates a status byte (1) or a data byte (0). Therefore, the first byte is a status byte that specifies a **note on** event (with the first four bits) on channel 1 (with the second four bits; remember what we said about MIDI channel 1 really being 0000 in binary). The second byte is a data byte, which in this case indicates decimal 60 or middle C (binary 0111100). The third byte is again a data byte, which indicates the standard value for a nonvelocity keyboard, decimal 64 (binary 01000000).

Hey! That wasn't so bad. If you want to know the exact formats of other MIDI words, you'll find this information in Appendix A.

For those who have had the perseverance to make it through this section, your payoff is at hand. You now know more about computers than many of the salespeople at computer stores, so give yourself a well-deserved pat on the back. Things get easier from here. Next chapter we'll talk about MIDI channels and how you can talk to 16 different devices over a single cable. Then we'll talk about the actual MIDI language and what it expresses, which is where matters start to become really interesting.

Chapter 3

Tuning in to MIDI Channels and MIDI Modes

Last chapter we learned that MIDI transmits and receives "information packets" that describe such musical events as whether a note is on or off, the amount of pitch bending being added to a note, and so on. All of this was always expressed in terms of a single channel and assumed that we were sending data to or from one specific keyboard.

However, MIDI can send and receive data over 16 different channels—each of which can carry unique data and drive its own polyphonic MIDI instrument. But how, you might wonder, can MIDI transmit 16 different channels over a single cord? After all, to send 16 different audio signals somewhere, you would need 16 different cords . . .

Ah, but remember that MIDI transmits *information*, not audio, and sends this data serially—in other words, each individual piece of information is sent consecutively. If we "tag" each piece of data with a channel identification number (ID), then we can program a particular MIDI instrument to look only for data that has a particular channel ID.

A good analogy would be sorting mail by zip code. Imagine a conveyor belt where each piece of mail goes past a mail sorter, one piece of mail at a time. As each letter goes by, it is scanned for its zip code; and letters are sorted into individual piles accordingly. MIDI works similarly. Each instrument monitors the MIDI data stream (analogous to the mail going past on the conveyor belt); and when an instrument detects data with the same channel ID number as the channel for which the instrument is programmed, it acts

on that information. For example, if a **note on** message is sent over channel 1, only those synthesizers tuned to channel 1 will receive this **note on** command. Devices tuned to other channels will ignore the data. This situation is also analogous to a television, which selects a particular channel for viewing out of the many signals coming down the antenna.

As we'll see later when discussing Mono mode, some instruments use more than one channel at a time. However, these devices still are considered tuned to a "basic" MIDI channel, and the other channels are related to this basic channel.

Connecting Multiple Instruments

As mentioned earlier, we need only one MIDI cord to transmit MIDI information from one instrument to another. However, the situation gets somewhat more complicated with more than two instruments. There are two popular methods of interconnecting multiple instruments via MIDI: *daisy-chaining* and *star networking*.

Daisy-chaining is particularly applicable to situations where one master keyboard controls a relatively small number of slave synthesizers (i.e., an onstage remote keyboard controls a bank of offstage slave synthesizers). This configuration makes good use of the MIDI Thru jack. **Fig. 3-1** shows four keyboards daisy-chained together, which is just about the maximum amount of keyboards you can reliably use in a daisy-chained network.

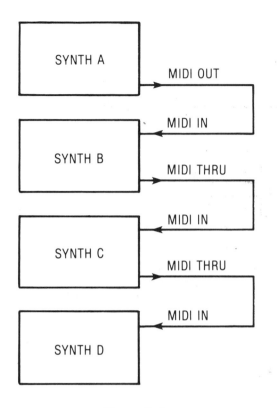

Figure 3-1

Synth A, the master, sends data through the MIDI Out jack to Synth B. Since we also want to control Synth C, and since (as mentioned in Chapter 1) Synth B's MIDI Thru jack sends a replica of the signal received at the MIDI In jack, patching Synth B's MIDI Thru jack to Synth C's MIDI In jack will carry Synth A's data to Synth C. Similarly, Synth C's MIDI Thru can send Synth A's data to Synth D.

Unfortunately, there are some problems with daisy-chaining. It takes a small but measurable amount of time for the components in a MIDI interface to respond to data, so sending data down a chain of more than three or four devices can lead to unpredictable results (called "data distortion") towards the end of the chain. A star network solves these kinds of problems for larger setups, since the MIDI signal doesn't endure the degradation associated with passing through multiple instruments. In **Fig. 3-2** a MIDI Thru *fan-out box* expands a single MIDI Out into four buffered MIDI Outs, which then feed four slave synths. By buffered, we mean that the MIDI signal is clean, strong, and capable of leaping tall buildings at a single

bound (or at least making its way through a pretty long MIDI cable length).

Now that we've got some gear hooked up, we should examine how synthesizers assign the note information received over a particular channel to their internal *voices*. A voice is the synthesizer's basic tone generating block. Polyphonic synthesizers contain multiple voices to allow for playing multiple notes (i.e., a six-voice polyphonic synthesizer can produce up to six notes simultaneously).

MIDI has four different modes for distributing data to synthesizer voices, which are made up of various combinations of three MIDI messages: Omni, Poly, and Mono. Omni on/off messages tell an instrument whether or not to respond to the information coming in on *all* 16 MIDI channels. Poly and Mono messages determine whether the instrument will respond polyphonically or monophonically. Now let's see what happens when we combine these messages.

Note: Mode operation is different for MIDI transmitters and MIDI receivers; we'll cover receivers first.

Mode 1: Omni On/Poly ("Omni mode")

In Mode 1, commonly called "Omni," the instrument receives notes being sent on all channels (1 through 16) and responds polyphonically. Thus, as note-on/off and other voice-related messages are received from any channel, they are assigned to the various synthesizer voices until all voices have been assigned. If additional data comes in, the synthesizer will usually "steal" the first voice played and assign the new data to this voice.

If you interconnect two synthesizers in Mode 1 via MIDI, the data being sent by the master will always be received by the slave. No channel assignment is necessary, since no matter which channel contains the transmitted data, the slave will respond to this data. An instrument in Mode 1 is like a player playing every part of a score on a single instrument. Originally, Omni mode was intended as a sort of "goof-proof" mode. However, now that musicians have become more knowledgeable about MIDI, Omni mode is not used all that much.

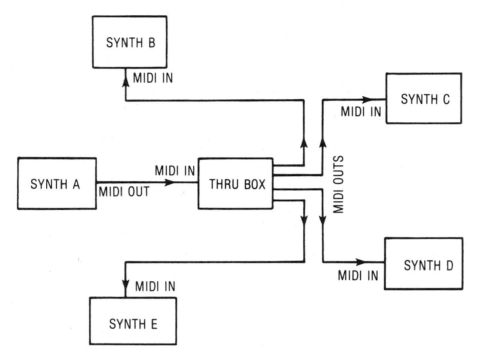

Figure 3–2

Mode 2: Omni On/Mono

This is similar to Mode 1, except that any information coming in on any channel is assigned to just *one* voice; therefore, the slave instrument responds monophonically. This mode produces the same kind of keyboard note assignment protocol as older monophonic analog synthesizers (minimoog, ARP Odyssey, etc.), where no matter how many keys you play only one note will sound. If the slave receives messages telling it to play more than one note at a time, the instrument will (depending on its design) play either the highest note, the lowest note, or the last note played. (Some synthesizers let you choose between these three "note priority" options.)

Mode 3: Omni Off/Poly ("Poly mode")

In this mode (commonly called "Poly mode"), Omni is off. Therefore, the slave no longer looks for information on all channels but instead looks for information coming in over one specific channel. Since Poly is on, the instrument will play polyphonically (and assigns its voices in the same manner as Mode 1). With Mode 3 you must select the

same channel for the transmitter and receiver. If, for example, the transmitter is sending data on channel 2 and the receiver is looking for data on channel 1, they will not be able to communicate. An instrument in Poly mode is like a player playing one particular instrument (including those instruments playing polyphonic parts) from a score.

Mode 4: Omni Off/Mono ("Mono mode")

And now for something completely different. Omni Off/Mono, also called "Mono mode," is a very powerful MIDI mode. But many people find it confusing, so pay close attention.

With Mode 4 selected, *each* synth voice is assigned to its own channel number. For example, with a six-voice synth tuned to basic channel 1, the first voice responds to the data coming in over channel 1, the second voice responds to the data coming in over channel 2, and so on until the sixth voice responds to the data coming in over channel 6. Synthesizers with multitimbral Mono capability also allow each voice to be set to its own sound program. Therefore, each channel can drive its own voice, ac-

Mono Limitations

One of the questions with Mono operation is whether messages transmitted from a master keyboard (such as pitch bend or modulation wheel) apply to all channels or just one channel. For example, Sequential gear assumes that pitch bend messages apply to all voices in a Mono instrument. This produces strange results when you hook up a guitar-to-MIDI converter in Mono mode, since bending one string will cause *all* voices to bend, not just the voice relating to the string being bent. This is also a problem with sequencers, since a pitch bend command on one track will "bleed over" into other tracks. While some instruments (such as the Oberheim Xpander) do allow for selectively enabling pitch bend and similar messages for particular voices, this can create other problems since sending individual pitch bend messages for each voice of a chord takes longer than sending a single "global" (applies to all channels) pitch bend message. This can create noticeable delays under some circumstances.

Mono mode remains one of the "grey areas" of MIDI, although manufacturers are trying to define this protocol further. In particular, Octave Plateau and SynthAxe, who both make MIDI guitar controllers, are very interested in resolving this situation in as elegant a manner as possible since Mono mode lends itself well to guitar.

cessed via MIDI, which can be programmed for its own timbre. However, there are some limitations involved with Mono mode (see sidebar).

Within the limitations mentioned in the sidebar, multitimbral synthesizers and MIDI sequencers make a great team, since a single instrument can produce several independent melody lines that respond to information coming in over different channels. Therefore, if the sequencer has a bass line programmed in sequencer track 1, a horn line programmed in track 2, and a violin solo programmed in track 3, you could send the data from track 1 to the multitimbral synth's first voice (which would be programmed for a bass sound, of course), the data from track 2 to the multitimbral synth's second voice (programmed for a horn sound), and the data from track 3 to the multitimbral synth's third voice (programmed for a violin sound). Since a single multitimbral instrument can provide multiple single-line melodies—each with its own timbre—it offers more flexibility than standard synthesizers. Chords can also be created by using more than one sequencer track and more than one instrument voice. In the example given above, sequencer tracks 4, 5, and 6 could be programmed for triads. Assigning these to voices 4, 5, and 6 of the multitimbral instrument—and setting voices 4, 5, and 6 for the same timbre—would produce chords where each note has the same timbre. **Fig. 3-3** summarizes this example.

Note that some synthesizers provide bitimbral operation by letting you split the keyboard into two (or more) sections, whereupon you can assign each half of the split to a different MIDI channel. For example, if the lower half of the split is set for a bass sound and the upper half of the split for a trumpet, each could be driven polyphonically from a separate sequencer track over separate MIDI channels. Some bitimbral synths can handle separate pitch bends for each side of the split, but others cannot. Controller capabilities, discussed in depth in the next chapter, is one of those areas that must be examined very closely before making any purchasing decision. Otherwise, severe frustration (and possibly insanity in unstable minds) can result.

That's the big picture on MIDI modes. However, so far we've only considered modes from the standpoint of a MIDI device *receiving* data. MIDI instruments that *transmit* data also have their own protocol in different modes.

MIDI Transmission Modes

A MIDI device transmitting in Mode 1 (Omni) transmits all voice data over the basic channel. The basic channel number is usually assignable; but if there is no provision to select channels, the device will transmit over channel 1. A device transmitting in Mode 2 will send voice messages for *one* voice over its basic channel. A device transmitting in Mode 3 (Poly) will send polyphonic voice messages for *all* available voices over the basic channel—just like Mode 1.

As with receiving, Mode 4 is a special case. If a six-voice synthesizer transmits in Mode 4 over basic channel 1, the voice messages for the first voice will be transmitted over channel 1, the voice messages for the

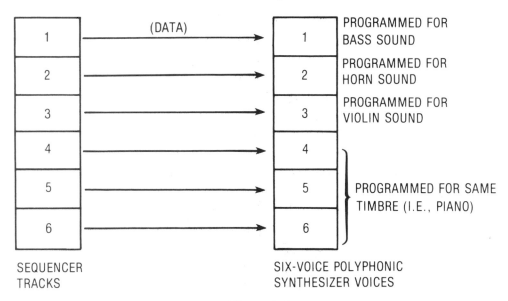

Figure 3-3

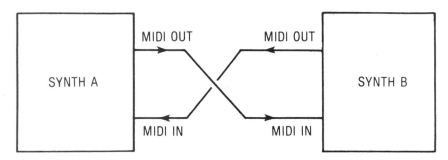

Figure 3-4

second voice will be transmitted over channel 2, and so on until the voice messages for the sixth voice will be transmitted over channel 6. An instrument in Mode 4 essentially transmits data over the same channels as those assigned to receive data.

Applications of Different Modes

We didn't just go over the above as an intellectual exercise by any means; each mode has specific advantages for particular applications. Note, however, that not all instruments are capable of all modes.

For instant slaving of keyboards, Omni (Mode 1) allows data transfer without having to think about channel assignments or other complications. If two synthesizers are in Omni mode, simply patching Synth A's MIDI Out to Synth B's MIDI In and Synth B's MIDI Out to Synth A's MIDI In (see **Fig. 3-4**) will let either synthesizer control the other synthesizer. So, playing on Synth A will trigger sounds from Synth A and B; playing on Synth B will trigger sounds from Synth B and A.

If you're into recording different polyphonic melody lines with a multichannel sequencer, Poly (Mode 3) lets you send the data for each channel to a specific instrument (or voice, with multitimbral instruments). This is like multichannel recording, where you assign one instrument to one track, another instrument to another track, and so on.

Although several sequencers allow you to program up to 16 individual parts and send this data to a like number of channels, very few people have 16 keyboards to hook up to their sequencers. Mono (Mode 4) to the rescue: Multitimbral keyboards set for Mode 4 can produce many different independent melody lines from a single instrument. Suppose you have two six-voice multitimbral synthesizers. Since each voice can be assigned to its own channel, you can have up to twelve individual tracks of sound. Granted, each track will only be one voice and not capable of polyphony. However, if you needed some chords, you could simply sacrifice some of the tracks (i.e., one of the six-voice synths could play two sets of triads and use up two MIDI channels; unfortunately, not many synths actually implement this feature). Also note that Mode 4 is practically a requirement for MIDI guitar con-trollers so that bends, slides, pull-offs, and the like occurring on one string are sent to *only* the voice assigned to that string.

Now that we know about modes and hooking up gear, let's delve into the mysteries of the MIDI language itself. We've already discussed some words (such as **note on** messages, **note off** messages, dynamics messages, and a few others); but MIDI has a far richer vocabulary than the few concepts we've presented so far . . . as we'll find out in the next chapter.

Chapter 4

The MIDI Language

Selecting MIDI Parameters

We have talked about selecting MIDI functions but have not really explained how these functions are selected. In most cases front panel controls do double duty as MIDI function/parameter select controls. As one example, if a synthesizer has a keypad for entering program numbers, you might select MIDI channel 16 by first pushing a switch that puts the instrument into MIDI mode, then keying in 16 on the keypad. Some instruments even include LCD displays to guide you through the MIDI setup process.

However, the number of available MIDI functions varies greatly from instrument to instrument. In fact, manufacturers periodically update some instruments—usually via a simple software change—to give new capabilities. (For this reason it has become more important than ever before to send in your warranty card so that you can be informed of any available updates.)

One very important point about the MIDI specification is that it sets no criteria for exactly what functions an instrument must include to call itself a MIDI instrument. An inexpensive synthesizer that responds solely to note on/off messages or a multithousand dollar synthesizer that includes a comprehensive set of MIDI functions may both be legitimately advertised as "MIDI-compatible." The only way to know for sure what an instrument can really do is to look over its *MIDI implementation* information (the MIDI equivalent of a "spec sheet"); this tells which functions are available (implemented) on the instrument and which ones aren't. For example, one instrument might be able to transmit and receive over all 16 channels, whereas another one might only be able to transmit over 1 channel but receive on all

16; the implementation sheet will provide this data.

In order to make sense out of a MIDI spec sheet, you need to know what the MIDI language covers. Then you can decide how fluently a device "speaks" MIDI . . . so let's get on with the language lesson. Later on, we'll give some examples of MIDI implementation sheets and how to read them.

Remember: Each of these MIDI messages consists of a status byte and data bytes. The status byte will always start off with four bits that identify the function. Since this occurs with each and every MIDI message, we won't repeat this fact when discussing individual messages. If you need to review the subject of status and data bytes, check the end of Chapter 2. If you're curious as to the actual binary format of the various status bytes, refer to Appendix A.

PART 1: CHANNEL VOICE MESSAGES

These are the messages that relate to the synthesizer voices: which notes are being played, the degree of pitch bend, keyboard velocity, and so on.

Note On

This message says to turn a specific note on and sends three pieces of data:

1. The channel number (1 to 16) in which the note should be turned on.
2. The key number of the note being turned on (0-127, with 0 being the lowest note, 127 the highest, and 60 being middle C).
3. The key velocity (0-127, with 0 being no velocity and 127 being maximum velocity). With nonvelocity keyboards the default

value is 64. The faster the key goes from the key-up to the key-down position (as determined by the dynamics of your playing), the greater the velocity value. If the velocity data controls a synthesizer's VCA, playing more dynamically increases the overall level.

Remember, these messages can be *polyphonic* for *each* channel. Even though note data is transmitted serially (one piece of data right after the other), the transmission rate is so rapid that multiple notes sent along a single software channel appear to be sounding simultaneously.

Also note that many MIDI instruments can neither receive nor transmit the entire available range of notes, and some devices may be able to receive more notes than they can transmit. Therefore, a MIDI implementation sheet should mention both the range of notes the keyboard can transmit and the range that can be received. (For example, the Casio CZ-101 can transmit notes 36-84 but receive notes 36-96—one extra octave.) Another possibility is that an instrument will simply transpose those notes outside its range; with the Poly 800 (a four-octave instrument) MIDIed to a five-octave master keyboard, playing on the master's top octave triggers the same notes on the Poly 800 as playing on the master's next-to-top octave. An instrument's MIDI implementation sheet should take note of this kind of thing, although not all do.

Note Off

This message turns a specific note off (as occurs when you lift your finger off a keyboard key) and sends three pieces of data:

1. The channel number (1 to 16) over which the note should be turned off.
2. The key number of the note being turned off (0-127, with 0 being the lowest note, 127 the highest, and 60 being middle C).
3. The key off (release) velocity (0-127, with 0 being no velocity and 127 being maximum velocity). This data indicates how fast you release the key, thus allowing your playing style to affect the duration of a note's release phase.

Polyphonic Key Pressure (Aftertouch)

Some MIDI keyboards respond not only to velocity but to pressure applied to the keyboard after the keys are down. Polyphonic key pressure sends three pieces of data:

1. The channel number (1 to 16) over which the pressure data should be sent.
2. The key number of the note being affected by the polyphonic key pressure (0-127, with 0 being the lowest note, 127 the highest, and 60 being middle C).
3. The key pressure value (0-127, with 0 being no pressure and 127 being maximum pressure).

Application: When playing a trumpet part, key pressure data could be used to raise the filter cutoff frequency; pressing harder would therefore simulate the sound of a musician pushing more air through a trumpet. With polyphonic key pressure, each key produces its own unique pressure signal. Thus, when playing a chord, pressing down on just one key affects only one note of the chord.

Note that keyboards with true polyphonic key pressure are complex, expensive, rare, and often difficult to service (although they are a joy to play). As a matter of economics, most pressure-sensitive keyboards offer overall pressure response (described next) instead of polyphonic key pressure.

Overall Pressure (Aftertouch)

Overall pressure is the pressure being applied to the keyboard from all notes being held down . . . sort of an "average pressure." This message sends the overall pressure for all notes in a given channel and consists of two pieces of data:

1. The channel number (1 to 16) over which the pressure data should be sent.
2. The channel pressure value (0-127, with 0 being no pressure and 127 being maximum pressure).

About Those MIDI Controllers . . .

Before learning more words of the MIDI language, we need to delve into the mysterious (at least initially) world of MIDI controllers. This detour will take some time, but that's only because we're dealing with a very important aspect of MIDI.

There's more to slaving synthesizers together than simply exchanging note information . . . such as modulation. Ideally, adding modulation (such as vibrato) to some parameter on the master should similarly modulate the slave; or if you turn on portamento, the slave should follow suit. (Pitch bending, another controller, is deemed so important that it has its own message apart from other controllers).

MIDI has provisions for sending and receiving data about 31 *controllers.* These can be often-used controllers (such as modulation wheel or filter cutoff) or more esoteric controllers (such as portamento amount, envelope generator lag time, etc.).

Note that all of the above are called "continuous" controllers; like a standard potentiometer, they cover a *continuous* range of values (unlike a controller such as an on/off switch, which only selects between two possible values). MIDI also makes provisions for 32 on/off switches and 29 undefined controllers.

These controllers can send and receive data in either *low-resolution* or *high-resolution* mode. From my experience low resolution, which quantizes the controller into 128 steps and requires one byte of data, seems to be the more common of the two modes. High resolution, which quantizes to over 16,000 different steps and requires two bytes of data, gives a smoother "feel" to controllers; but it transmits more data, eats up more memory space, and "clogs" the MIDI data stream.

To accommodate sending controller information between instruments, MIDI has 128 available controller numbers (we'll cover the actual manner in which data is transferred in a little bit). You can think of these as 128 minichannels within each main channel. These mini-channels transmit and receive controller change data (such as modulation, whether the sustain footswitch is on or off, etc.). Each continuous controller, in low-resolution mode, is assigned a controller number from 0 to 31; in high-resolution mode, the additional data byte required for high-resolu-

tion operation appears over controller numbers 32-63 (note that this data is required *in addition* to data occurring over controller numbers 0-31). Controller numbers 64-95 carry switch information (on/off), and controller numbers 96-122 are at present undefined. We'll talk about controller numbers 123-128 toward the end of this section.

So how does all this fit together? Well, for one example let's take a look at modulation. When you add modulation on a master synth, the master sends data (labeled as controller number 1) over the selected MIDI basic channel; the controller data tells how much modulation has been added. If the slave synth's modulation circuitry is checking for data from controller number 1 (which, according to the MIDI spec, it should be), then the two controllers will "talk" to each other and adding modulation on the master will add modulation on the slave.

That sounds simple enough, but there are some complications. First of all, most controllers are officially undefined. So, if Synth A assigns portamento time information to controller number 5 and Synth B listens for portamento time information over controller number 8, the portamento data will not be transferred from Synth A to Synth B. (However, note that if Synth B has some other function—not necessarily portamento—listening to controller number 5, that function will be controlled by channel A's portamento time information.) While this lack of nonstandardization would at first appear to be an unbearable limitation, two trends are of great help.

First, some de facto standards are emerging. The modulation wheel is officially controller 1, and the damper (sustain) footswitch is officially controller 64. In addition, the overwhelming popularity of the DX-7 has created several de facto standards. Here's a chart of the current standard as of this writing:

The second important trend is that many MIDI instruments now include *assignable controllers* so that *any* controller can be assigned to *any* controller number (usually accomplished via punching front panel buttons). Not only does this approach solve the problem of controller number incompatibility, it allows for some nifty tricks. For example,

Parameter	Controller Number
Modulation wheel	1
Breath controller	2
Pressure	3[a]
Foot pedal	4
Portamento time	5
Slider (data entry knob)	6
Main volume	7
Damper (sustain) switch	64
Portamento on/off switch	65
Sustenuto on/off switch	66[b]
Soft on/off switch	67[b]
Data + (DX-7 + button)	96
Data − (DX-7 − button)	97

[a] This applies to older DX-7s only; this controller number is unused on newer models.

[b] These controller numbers are used by Roland.

suppose you want a slave synth's filter cutoff to follow the master synth's modulation wheel. If the filter cutoff can be assigned to various controller numbers, you would simply assign it to listen to controller number 1. As the master sends out modulation data tagged as controller number 1, the slave would use this information to control the filter cutoff.

In some cases controllers can transmit, as well as receive, over particular controller numbers. This feature can help you determine which controllers on a slave correspond to which controller numbers on a master. The procedure is to set up a patch on the slave, then select a footpedal, slide pot, or modulation wheel as a controller at the master synth. With the master's controller assigned to controller number 1, varying this controller should vary the slave's modulation. Next, assign other controller numbers to the footpedal, slide pot, or modulation wheel. Perhaps selecting controller number 7 and varying the controller will affect the slave's level, or maybe selecting controller number 5 and varying the controller will affect the slave's portamento time. Keep track of which slave functions respond to particular controller numbers on the master.

If an instrument does not have assignable controllers, the owner's manual should tell you which functions are expecting data from which controller numbers. However, there are often *unimplemented functions* which are not listed in the manual but can nonetheless be controlled by selecting the proper controller number. As you experiment, make notes of any controllable functions not listed in the manual for future reference.

Even assignable controllers do not solve all problems, however. Often the amount of pitch bend between two synths may not track; for example, bending up a fifth on the master may result in the slave bending up a third or some other interval. In theory, sensitivity is supposed to be full range in the transmitter and adjustable (if at all) in the receiver; but this is not universally applied. Besides, even when the range is adjustable, there's no guarantee that the *taper*—the rate of change—is constant from one instrument to another. Therefore, even though the maximum and minimum amounts of pitch bend might coincide, tracking might not be perfect in intermediate ranges. Fortunately, for small amounts of pitch bend, improper tracking is not necessarily a problem; in fact, it can even impart a "thicker" sound since as the two tones spread apart they will create choruslike effects.

Well . . . so much for controllers. If this doesn't make complete sense now, don't worry about it. Play with some MIDI instruments for a while, then come back and read this; it should all fall into place.

Now, on with our language lesson.

Control Change

The *control change* word comprises three pieces of data:

1. The channel number (1 to 16) over which the controller data should be sent.
2. The controller number (0-127, as described previously).
3. The controller value. In low-resolution mode, this is 0-127, with 0 being full off and 127 being full on. High resolution sends an additional value of 0-127, thus providing 128 steps in between each step of low-resolution mode. For an analogy think of low resolution as sending the time in minutes, and high resolution as providing additional information on the number of seconds. Although high resolution is a great idea in theory, in practice there are some serious problems (see sidebar).

The Problem With High Resolution

The seven bits of data containing the low-resolution information are referred to as the MSB (most significant bits), while the seven bits of data containing the high-resolution information are referred to as the LSB (least significant bits). As mentioned earlier, the MSB data for various controllers appears as controller numbers 0-31, while the LSB data for various controllers appears as controller numbers 32-63. According to the MIDI specification, only the LSB is transmitted for small changes, and only the MSB when no LSB is being used. But now let's look at what happens when you use both, taking pitch bend as an example.

If the LSB changes by a small amount, the computer registers the new bend value immediately. If the change is larger, there's a brief glitch when the LSB changes, followed by the MSB being received and acted upon. When changing the data value from 1000000 1111111 to 1000001 0000000, the data changes as follows:

```
1000000 1111111
1000000 0000000
1000001 0000000
```

. . . which produces a very audible glitch.

Another problem is that it takes four to six bytes to send the complete message. By restricting the bend message to three bytes (two in some situations), the response is much faster, the MIDI buss doesn't get clogged with extra bytes, and it takes a lot less memory to store pitch bend data in a sequencer.

With regard to controllers in general, many people in the industry feel that the high resolution controller numbers (32-63) are more or less useless and should be allocated to other, more useful functions.

Pitch Bend

The *pitch bend* word comprises two pieces of data.

1. The channel number (1 to 16) over which the controller data should be sent.
2. The pitch bend value. The pitch bend data can be sent in either low-resolution mode (with seven bits, or 128 steps, of resolution; 64 corresponds to no pitch bend) or in high-resolution mode, as described above.

Program Change (Also Called "Program Select")

Slave instruments that have **program change** selected (enabled) will respond to program changes at the master. The **program change** message consists of two pieces of data:

1. The channel number (1 to 16) over which the program change should occur.
2. The selected program number (1 out of 128 possibilities).

Applications: Suppose you have selected a cello sound on the master and a violin sound on the slave, and that if you change the master program to a trumpet, you want the slave program to change to saxophone. To do this, you would enable **program select** on the slave so that it would respond to program change information (disabling **program change** means that the slave will stay on the same program until changed manually).

With sequencers, **program change** messages can usually be recorded on a channel along with note information. On playback these messages will cause all MIDI-compatible instruments tuned to that channel (assuming **program change** is enabled) to change programs.

This all sounds wonderful, but the catch is a lack of consistency in the way manufacturers number programs. Programs might be numbered sequentially (1, 2, 3, 4, etc.) or arranged as banks of programs (A1 through A8, B1 through B8, etc.). There is also no standardization between which kinds of sounds correspond to particular program numbers; and given the nature of electronic devices, I don't think this is possible (a synthesizer provides too many sounds to be so easily categorized). Therefore, to use **program change** to best advantage, draw up a chart of which slave programs are selected when you change programs on the master. Then, you can copy programs on the slave from unsuitable memory locations to memory locations that are compatible with programs on the master (we'll give an example of how to do this in just a bit).

Also note that not all instruments allow for 128 programs. Therefore, if your master synth has 64 programs and your slave 100, you may not be able to access programs 65-

100 on the slave from the master. Then again, selecting program 65 from the master might "wrap around" back to program 1 on the slave . . . this type of information is supposed to be documented in MIDI implementation sheets, but you may have to really look for it.

Incidentally, some high-end synths (Voyetra, Xpander, and probably others) have program "steppers" that respond to MIDI **program change** commands. Each step calls up a particular program, usually including split and/or doubling combinations. Thus, if you are playing a song where you first call up program 36, then 12, then 62, and finally 43, you can arrange the stepper so that the first step selects program 36, the second step program 12, the third step program 62, and so on. When playing live, a master MIDI keyboard can send the **program change** commands that select different steps on the slave(s). This makes it very easy to have multiple slaves, each programmed to produce compatible sounds when a particular step is called up.

For those synths that do not include steppers, there are other ways to call up the desired slave program when you select a particular program on the master keyboard. Suppose two synths have the following programs stored in memory locations 1 through 6:

	Synth A	Synth B
1	Flute	Electric Piano
2	Trumpet	Organ
3	Saxophone	Clavinet
4	Strings	Strings
5	Guitar	Vox humana
6	Organ	Helicopter sound effect

If Synth A is the master and you choose program 6 (organ), Synth B will play a helicopter. Unless you're working on the soundtrack for *Apocalypse Now*, this is probably not going to be all that musically useful a combination. On the other hand, choosing master program 4 selects a string program on both synthesizers, which might be useful in creating a fuller string sound than either instrument can provide by itself.

To make up a collection of musically compatible programs, you would need to move programs around by copying and erasing programs (consult your owner's manual)

so that selecting programs on Synth A produces the desired program changes on Synth B. Let's suppose you want the flute on A doubled with the vox humana on B, the trumpet on A doubled with the strings on B, the clavinet on B all by itself, the strings on A doubled with strings on B, the guitar on A by itself, and the organ on A doubled with the clavinet on B. Copying Synth B's programs to new locations and erasing unwanted programs can produce the following setup:

	Synth A	Synth B
1	Flute	Vox humana
2	Trumpet	Strings
3	*	Clavinet
4	Strings	Strings
5	Guitar	*
6	Organ	Clavinet

The programs marked with * are *null programs*, where the synthesizer makes no sound. To create a null program, select control settings that disable the synthesizer's sound making capabilities (i.e., turn the VCA all the way off or the filter all the way down).

"But," you say, "my slave synth doesn't number the programs sequentially. In fact, it groups programs as eight banks of eight programs, like 1-1 through 1-8, 2-1 through 2-8, 3-1 through 3-8, and so on. How do I know which slave synth program will be called up when I select a particular program number on the master?"

Now is the time to get out a paper and pencil and check how selecting programs on the master affects the slave. (Take notes of your setup as you go along—it will save you a lot of time and frustration later.) You will probably notice some kind of correlation. For example, I was slaving an Oberheim Xpander (which numbers programs sequentially starting with 00) to a Roland GR-700 (which groups programs as eight banks of eight). After reaching deep into my brain for recollections of high school math, I figured out the following equation to convert GR-700 program numbers to Xpander program numbers:

1. Multiply the selected GR-700 *bank* number by 8.
2. Add the GR-700 *program* number, then subtract nine.

Expressed as a formula, this would be . . .

(GR bank $\times$ 8) + (GR program number)
-9 = Xpander program number

Example: Calling up program 4-3 (bank 4, program 3) on the GR-700 will call up program $(4 \times 8) + 3 - 9 = 26$ on the Xpander.

Of course, trial-and-error will also work, but figuring out a conversion formula will probably save you time in the long run. In any event, it is *your* responsibility to make sure that program changes on the master produce the desired results on your slave machines.

Note that a similar situation can occur with the **song select** function; your drum machine might number its patterns differently

from your sequencer. Again, either determine the correlation between the two by trial-and-error, or figure out a formula.

Don't let this talk of incompatibility scare you off, though; you'll be able to figure things out with a little work. **Program change** is a very useful command, and each successive generation of MIDI instruments implements the **program change** function in more powerful ways.

PART 2: CHANNEL MODE MESSAGES

These messages affect the channel's mode of operation. They are all special cases of the **control change** message discussed previously.

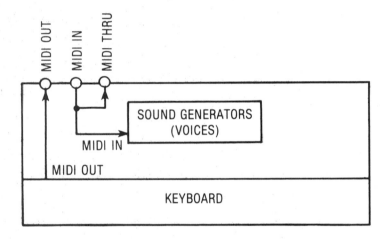

MIDI SIGNAL ROUTING WITH LOCAL CONTROL *OFF*

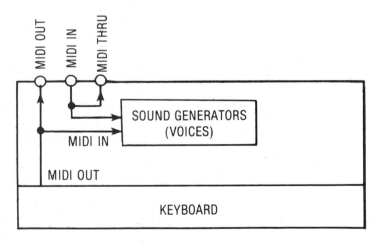

MIDI SIGNAL ROUTING WITH LOCAL CONTROL *ON*

Figure 4-1

Local/Remote Keyboard Control

This message is designed for "integrated" synths that contain a keyboard, modulation wheels, etc. (the controllers) along with sound-generating circuitry (the voices). Referring to **Fig. 4-1**, in the *on* (local mode) position, controller data (key presses, pitch bends, and the like) goes directly to the voice circuitry and also appears at the MIDI Out. With local control *off* (remote mode), the controller data appears solely through MIDI Out, and the voices respond solely to data received at MIDI In. In other words, **local control off** disconnects the direct path between the controllers and voice circuitry. This message comprises three pieces of data and has the same data format as the controller messages:

1. The channel number (1 to 16) being subject to local/remote control.
2. The controller number (122) that identifies the message as pertaining to the local control function.
3. Whether local control is on or off.

Application: Local on/off can turn an "integrated" keyboard synth into a separate master keyboard and expander module for use with other (keyboardless) expander modules or with external MIDI data proces-

sors (such as MIDI arpeggiators or data delay lines). For example, suppose you have a MIDI arpeggiator that accepts MIDI In chord data and converts this data to a MIDI Out signal consisting of arpeggiated notes. With **local control off**, you will hear the arpeggios *without* hearing the block chords from which the arpeggios are derived; with **local control on**, you will hear the block chords. Note that more voices are available for arpeggiation effects with **local control off**, since you're not using up voices to play the original block chord.

Application: When programming a sequencer, with **local control off** you can record a new part through an expander into the sequencer while playing back an earlier part on the internal voice circuitry (see **Fig. 4-2**).

Application: When slaving instruments together, you normally hear the master and slave simultaneously; but there might be occasions when you would want to hear just one or the other. To hear the slave keyboard(s) only, turn **local control off** (remote mode) at the master; this disables any sound-generating circuitry associated with the master, but any slaves "downstream" of the master's MIDI Out will continue to be controlled by the master keyboard. (Incidentally, inter-

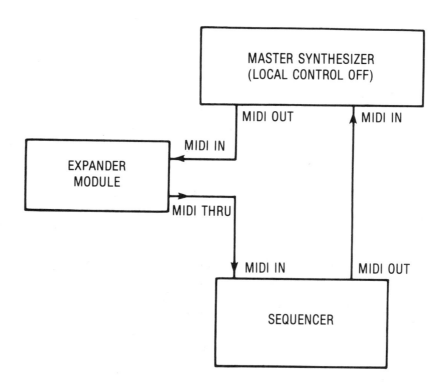

Figure 4-2

rupting MIDI data going to the slave in order to hear only the master keyboard is a somewhat more complex operation. Either disconnect the MIDI cord, use a MIDI switch as described in Chapter 9, or assign the slave to a different channel from the master if both synths are in Poly mode.)

All Notes Off

This is the "shut up" request and consists of three pieces of data:

1. The channel number (1 to 16) over which the notes should be turned off.
2. The controller number (123) that identifies the message as the **all notes off** message.
3. A "dummy" byte that pads the length out to three bytes. The dummy byte is necessary because *all* controller messages are three bytes long (this simplifies decoding the MIDI data stream, thus making the software easier to write).

Application: Suppose you're sending MIDI data from a sequencer to a keyboard and stop the sequencer in the middle of the sequence. All notes which had not received **note off** messages would be stuck on; sending the **all notes off** message (usually selected by pressing a button) will turn these notes off.

Unfortunately, the MIDI specification states that **all notes off** messages are optional and need not be honored—which makes the whole concept of these commands rather pointless, since you can't count on them to work in all cases.

Omni/Poly/Mono Select

Most MIDI instruments allow for more than one mode of operation (Omni, Poly, and Mono, though these are not all available simultaneously); and when acting as slaves, they can receive messages that switch the instrument to one of the available modes. Changing modes frequently issues an **all notes off** command so that the instrument will start off in its newly selected mode "from scratch." The data format is similar to the format for other controllers:

1. The channel number (1 to 16) being affected by the message.

2. The appropriate controller number (124 for **Omni off**, 125 for **Omni on**, 126 for **Mono on**, and 127 for **Poly on**) that identifies the mode being selected.
3. A third byte of data, which is 0 for messages 123 (**all notes off**), 124, 125, and 127. With Mono mode (message 126), the third byte indicates the number of channels to be allocated for mono data. Channels are numbered with the "basic channel" already established for that unit; for example, a Casio CZ-101 set to basic channel 4 would respond to mono data on channels 4, 5, 6, and 7 after receiving a **Mono on: 4** controller message.

PART 3: SYSTEM COMMON MESSAGES (ALL CHANNELS)

Some messages apply to *all* channels. These convey information such as song selection, how many measures have elapsed since a sequence started playing, and so on. Since **system common** messages affect the entire system, they do not carry any channel information.

Many of these messages are not implemented in existing machines, but they are available and defined for future use. As MIDI develops, instruments will surely become more and more MIDI-capable.

Song Position Pointer

A MIDI sequencer or drum machine can keep track of how many MIDI beats (up to a maximum of 16,384 beats; one MIDI beat = one sixteenth note) have elapsed since the sequence was started. The **song position pointer** message sends out a status byte plus two bytes that specify the count in sixteenth notes since the start of the song.

Application: Suppose a sequencer capable of sending song pointer information feeds a drum machine capable of receiving song pointer information. If you select a certain place as the start point, both units will automatically position (*auto-locate*) themselves to that start point. Pushing **play** will cause both units to start playing from the beginning of the specified measure.

Note that without **song pointer** information it would be necessary to start both the sequencer and drum machine at the beginning of the song, since one device would not know where it was with respect to the other except at the very beginning. (Once started, they would maintain sync by virtue of being driven by the same timing reference.)

Although the concept of a song pointer works well in theory, MIDI does not specify a minimum time between sending out a song position pointer (which stops the sequence so that the various devices can auto-locate) and continuing a sequence. (The **continue** message is described later; it is used after sending a **song pointer** message to cause a sequencer/drum machine to start playing from the indicated point.) Although some devices can auto-locate almost instantaneously upon receiving the **song pointer** information, other devices (especially those with high clock resolution) may take a while longer. Therefore, if a sequence is restarted immediately after the **song position pointer** information is sent, all is well if the units have managed to auto-locate themselves prior to being told to restart. Otherwise . . . trouble.

Also note that a surprisingly small number of devices actually implement the **song pointer** feature. Hopefully this situation will be remedied with future equipment.

Song Select

This message is conceptually similar to **program select** but selects 1 of 128 song numbers. The message consists of a status byte and a single data byte that specifies a song number from 0 to 127.

Application: Drum machines usually combine individual rhythm patterns to make a complete song, and sequencers group tracks together to make a complete song. Sending a **song select** message from a master keyboard, sequencer, or computer will cause the drum machine and sequencer to select songs with the specified number. (Note, however, that not all devices are capable of receiving **song select** information; and songs are not necessarily numbered in a consistent manner from machine to machine.) It is your responsibility to make sure that the sequencer and drum machine call up compatible programs upon receiving **song select** messages.

Tune Request

Pressing the **auto-tune** button found on many synthesizers will automatically tune the instrument according to an internal reference (usually A = 440 Hz). Sending a **tune request** message over MIDI does the equivalent of pushing all the instrument **auto-tune** buttons simultaneously. This message consists solely of the status byte.

Note that auto-tuned instruments are not guaranteed to be in tune with each other, even though they are in tune with themselves. **Tune request** does not actually tune the instruments; it just tells the instruments to tune themselves.

System Exclusive

Different manufacturers will always have different needs and objectives for their equipment, which is why the **system exclusive** message was invented. This message allows information unique to one manufacturer to be transmitted to, or received from, instruments made by the same manufacturer.

The first byte (status byte) alerts the system that a **system exclusive** message is about to occur. Next comes the manufacturer's identification number (0-127); *only equipment with this identification number will respond to the message.* The *use* of **system exclusive** messages is not limited to any one manufacturer. A computer program, for example, could send out different data to E-mu, Yamaha, and Roland equipment. Once **system exclusive** messages have been made public (via owner's manuals, bulletins, etc.), they cannot be changed—even by the original issuers—and anyone can use them.

Next comes a set of data bytes, which can represent a variety of data (such as the contents of a synthesizer's memory). This data can be transferred between compatible instruments or stored in a computer for further manipulation. **System exclusive** data forms the basis for using home computers as mass storage devices for synthesizers. We'll cover how this works in detail under MIDI Applications (Chapter 6).

After the data has been sent, the **system exclusive** process ends with an **end of system**

exclusive message. **System exclusive** activity can also be ended with a **reset** command (to be described soon); in fact, any status byte—except for the real time commands covered in the next section—can terminate a system exclusive.

As of this writing, there is a trend towards standardizing certain **system exclusives**, particularly those relating to text transmission, digitized audio samples, and bulk program dumps. However, nothing has been standardized at this point.

PART 4: SYSTEM REAL-TIME MESSAGES (ALL CHANNELS)

System real-time messages synchronize drum machines, sequencers, and other rhythmic-oriented devices. These messages start and stop timing-sensitive devices on the same beat, make sure they all follow the same system clock, and so on. **System real-time** messages are dropped into the data stream as required and have priority over other messages in order to maintain proper synchronization at all times. (If necessary, **real-time** messages can even be inserted *in between* bytes of other messages, provided that these other messages consist of two or more bytes.) Note that because **system real-time** messages affect the entire system, they do not carry channel data. Also note that these messages consist of a single status byte and no data bytes.

System Reset

A **system reset** command puts all MIDI equipment back to "square one"—the settings they have when they first receive power. For example, if when you first turn on a particular synthesizer it selects a certain set of parameters (program number, possibly degree of pitch bend, MIDI mode, and the like), then transmitting a **system reset** will cause that synthesizer to select those same parameters. In most cases, **system reset** is sent out from the MIDI master to the other MIDI devices. Thus, all instruments can be reset from a single master keyboard.

Application: One problem in live performance is that buttons can be accidentally pushed between sound-check time and show time. To solve this problem, program all instruments so that, upon power-up, they contain the programs and other parameters used in the first song. Then, just before starting the performance, send a **system reset** to insure that everything starts out with the correct settings.

Not all MIDI devices accept a **reset** message. For example, many floppy-disk-based instruments make no sound on power-up since they require that sound data be loaded from disk. Resetting such a device would leave the musician with no sound, so these instruments generally do not accept **reset** messages.

Timing Clock

The MIDI device that determines system timing (typically a drum machine or sequencer) sends out a *continuous* 24 pulses per quarter note timing reference to which the various slave devices synchronize. (Note that these are not really click-type pulses, as we discussed back in Chapter 1, but rather, MIDI clock data messages.) Since the **timing clock** message is continuous—regardless of whether a **stop**, **start**, or other message has been sent—different devices can establish good synchronization with the timing reference prior to receiving a **start** message. (Before the adoption of the MIDI 1.0 "official" spec, **timing clock** messages were handled somewhat differently; however, all modern MIDI equipment follows the protocol described above.)

Note: There should be only one master clock in a system so that all devices have a common timing reference.

Start From First Measure

Pressing **play** on the device that sets the system timing automatically sends out the **start from first measure** message to other MIDI devices. This message tells other sequencers and drum machines to return to the beginning of the song, then begin playing as soon as they receive the first **timing clock** data. This command therefore allows different units to all start together; **timing clock** messages then maintain synchronization throughout the duration of a composition. **Start from first measure** also resets the song pointer, if present, to 0.

Stop

Sending this message from the master will immediately stop all other timing-sensitive devices at the exact instant when they receive the command. You then have three options: press **start** on the master, which returns all devices back to the beginning and restarts the composition; continue the song from the point where stopped (as described shortly); or select a completely different song and start that.

Continue Start

Sending a **continue start** message, typically by hitting a **continue** switch on the system master, will allow all slave devices to resume playing a sequence or drum pattern from where they were last stopped.

Applications: As indicated earlier in the song pointer section, the major use of **continue** is to restart a sequence after a **song pointer** message has been sent. This is necessary because sending a **song pointer** will stop the sequence and cause any song pointer-compatible devices to auto-locate to the desired point in a song. Hopefully, the **continue** message will be sent after, and not before, all devices have auto-located themselves.

A different application involves working out material with a band; a song may be stopped temporarily while the songwriter describes upcoming chord progressions, lyrics, etc.

Active Sensing

This optional message solves a problem that was discovered shortly after MIDI was first defined. If a MIDI device sends a **note on** command to a MIDI slave and the MIDI connection becomes interrupted (say, because someone trips over the MIDI cord and pulls it out of the instrument), no **note off** commands will be received by the slave and it will keep playing the "stuck" note until someone resets the instrument. This can certainly

spoil your showcase gig for that A & R person who was almost ready to sign the band.

Active sensing works by sending out a message whenever there is no activity on the MIDI line. Any slaves equipped to receive this message will go into their **active sensing** state (sort of like a trance); as long as the slaves receive the **active sensing** message, or other MIDI activity, all works as expected. Should the **active sensing** messages cease and no other activity occurs on the MIDI line—which would be the case if the MIDI cord became disconnected or otherwise defective—then the slave will turn off its soundmaking circuitry (i.e., the voices in a synthesizer) to prevent stuck notes.

These days, **active sensing** is not used very much. Early DX-7s required **active sensing**; current DX-7s with updated software can get along perfectly well without it. Although **active sensing** is basically a good idea, the tradeoff is more clogging of the MIDI data stream, which is more of a problem than the problem addressed by **active sensing**.

* * * * *

So there you have it—the complete MIDI vocabulary, at least as of this writing. MIDI's expandability is a good news/bad news situation: The good news is that we can expect additional functions to be added as the world of MIDI matures. The bad news is that I'll have to constantly revise this book (which drives publishers nuts) to reflect any changes and you'll have to pay close attention to the latest MIDI news if you want to stay on top of things. Still, I feel that the advantages of an expandable, "living" specification outweigh the disadvantages of a spec that allows for no change or growth.

As noted earlier, not all MIDI devices implement all aspects of the MIDI spec. For example, most keyboard synthesizers will not send out **timing reference** messages, because they are melodic rather than rhythmic devices. However, a sophisticated synthesizer with an on-board sequencer might very well be able to serve as a master clock to which slave devices can synchronize.

These equipment differences emphasize the importance of studying a MIDI spec sheet to see exactly what a given piece of gear can or cannot do. Suppose that you want to use a remote keyboard to drive a number of off-stage MIDI slave synthesizers. If the slaves can accept velocity information, then to get the most out of the slaves the remote should be able to transmit velocity information. *Remember, an instrument doesn't have to implement all aspects of MIDI to be considered a MIDI instrument.* The situation is not unlike cassette recorders, where some units have Dolby B noise reduction, some dbx, and some Dolby C. If you have a bunch of Dolby B tapes, it's your responsibility to choose a cassette deck with Dolby B noise reduction. If you have both Dolby B and dbx tapes, then you need to find a machine that offers both types of noise reduction or to pick a machine that only offers one type of noise reduction and then purchase an accessory unit that lets you play the other kind of tapes.

Hey . . . no one said this would be easy. Using MIDI to its maximum potential means that you're going to have to think, and ask questions, and look over data sheets, and maybe even call a company's customer service number on occasion. But playing an instrument isn't easy, and you've managed to do that . . . and hopefully this book will teach you enough to ask the right kind of questions. Eventually, you will gain the experience that turns *you* into an expert. Besides, it's fun playing mad scientist and hooking MIDI equipment together to see what it can, and cannot, do.

So much for the pep talk. Let's check out some typical MIDI products and what kind of implementations you can expect to find with those products.

Chapter 5

Typical MIDI Implementations and Products

How extensive a MIDI implementation can you expect to find in a typical piece of MIDI gear? Read on and find out. First, though, there are a couple of cautions.

The music industry is like the fashion industry: every year companies introduce their new summer and winter styles. As a result, the products chosen as typical products for this section will be out of date relatively soon. Nonetheless, it's important to give an idea of what MIDI capabilities are built into "real-world" products and, also, to stress some of the points that make a unit particularly interesting or clever.

Although I've had extensive personal experience with some of the gear mentioned in this chapter, for other devices all I had to go on was a manufacturer's implementation sheet—which is subject to change without notice. In fact, even though all this information was checked with the manufacturers prior to publication, *any* MIDI product is subject to change without notice since manufacturers frequently add new features via software updates.

And of course, it's impossible to cover everything there is to know about a product in a few paragraphs, so the following descriptions touch on only the most pertinent MIDI-related features. Use this chapter to get a general idea of what's going on in MIDI-land; but before making any kind of buying decision, check with the manufacturer for current specifications and availability.

End of fine print . . . on with the show.

The MIDI Master Keyboard

MIDI has rekindled a great deal of interest in semimodular synthesizer systems—where the keyboard and sound-generating electronics are separated. This makes good economic sense since a keyboard is expensive; you should not be forced to replace it if you want to upgrade only the sound-generating capabilities.

Several companies now make master keyboards (also called "mother keyboards") of varying degrees of complexity. Some are designed for simple remote work and transmit note on/off, **program change**, and modulation data for one or two modulation controls (often assignable to different controller numbers). More sophisticated keyboards include such features as velocity, aftertouch, multiple assignable modulation controls, and **song select** for calling up sequences from the keyboard.

Naturally, more features mean more expense. The most expensive features are the ones that add physical control over the keyboard—aftertouch, velocity, release velocity, and the like. Therefore, these are the features which are often not implemented with inexpensive master keyboards.

Typical Product: Oberheim Xk

Oberheim has traditionally been known for making versatile products, and the Xk is no exception. Its multiple features let you control an entire MIDI system (i.e., drum machine, sequencer, and other keyboards) from this one unit.

The Xk keyboard (**Fig. 5-1**) spans five octaves and includes attack velocity, release velocity, and aftertouch. Other controllers— each of which can be assigned to any MIDI controller number—include a pitch bend lever, "double" modulation lever (so called

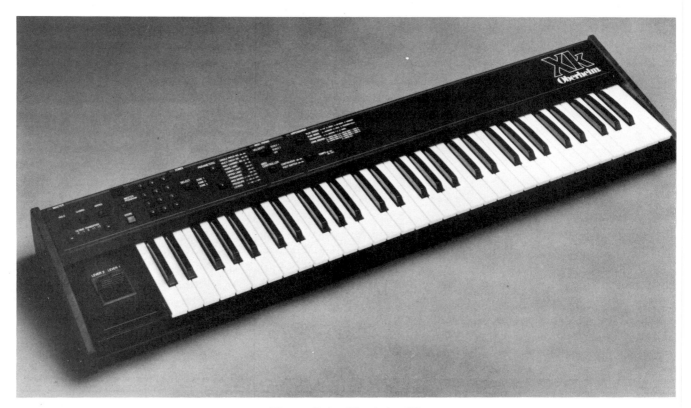

Figure 5-1. *Oberheim Xk*

because the center-to-front and center-to-back lever motions can be assigned independently to different controller numbers), slide pot, and footswitch input (typically used as a sustain pedal). The slide pot is a convenient way to check out what parameters a slave keyboard can receive; simply move the slide pot after selecting a controller number, and see how the slave's sound changes. Note that you might have to change programs on the slave occasionally in case some of the MIDI-controllable parameters are not present in all the programs.

The Xk keyboard can split into three different zones. This concept confuses a lot of people, but zoning simply allows you to subdivide the keyboard into multiple keyboards with smaller ranges. For example, suppose you want the Xk's *lowest* octave to trigger bass program 20 on slave Synth A over MIDI channel 6, the *middle* three octaves to trigger electric piano program 32 on Synth B over MIDI channel 7, and the *highest* octave to trigger brass program 17 on Synth C over MIDI channel 8. No problem . . . simply assign the first zone to the lowest octave, the second zone to the middle three octaves, and the third zone to the top octave (**Fig. 5-2**).

Each zone can have independent assignments for several parameters, including program number, MIDI channel, mono mode on/off, transposition, pressure on/off, levers on/off, and others. Thus, you can control three independent synthesizers from a single keyboard by playing in the zones controlling those keyboards. If desired, two or three zones can overlap for doubling or tripling effects respectively.

Program selection chooses from 100 master programs. Each program stores all settings in all three zones (as well as many other parameters). Thus, selecting a single program on the Xk can select three different programs on three different synths over three different MIDI channels.

For work with rhythm machines and sequencers, the Xk can transmit start/stop and **song select** messages. Other features include an on-board five-mode arpeggiator (with external clock input) and a chord hold.

Typical Product: Roland Axis-1

The Axis-1 is a 7-lb. remote keyboard that can be strapped on like a guitar. Its 45-key keyboard is velocity and pressure sensitive.

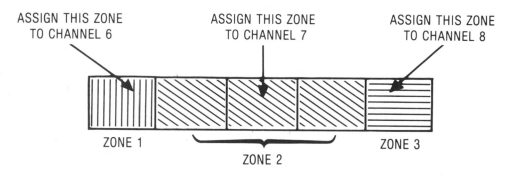

ASSIGN THIS ZONE
TO CHANNEL 6

ASSIGN THIS ZONE
TO CHANNEL 7

ASSIGN THIS ZONE
TO CHANNEL 8

ZONE 1

ZONE 2

ZONE 3

Figure 5-2

MIDI data can be transmitted over any of the 16 available channels.

There are three "wheel" controllers: pitch bend, master volume, and modulation. The latter two can be assigned to any MIDI controller number from 0 to 31.

Basic program selection chooses any one of 128 different programs on the slave synthesizer (assuming, of course, that the slave itself can store 128 different programs). *Patch chain*, a more complex feature, memorizes up to 10 combinations of program change number, key transposition, MIDI channel, and mode (Omni on/off, Poly, and Mono). As one example, the first patch (program) of the patch chain could send MIDI information over channel 2 to a synthesizer set to listen to channel 2 and could select a particular program on that synthesizer as well. The second patch could send MIDI information over channel 3 to a synthesizer set to listen to channel 3 and select a different program, along with a particular keyboard transposition.

Finally, four switches—octave up, modulation, remote pedal, and chord memory (which stacks the notes of a chord on a single key)—can be assigned to any of the switch controller numbers (64 to 95). Therefore, these switches can be custom-programmed to work optimally with a particular MIDI setup. Incidentally, once you've programmed all these various functions, controller numbers, and patch chains, don't worry about losing them if the power goes off; there's an internal battery back-up.

Polyphonic Synthesizer Implementation

As with all other MIDI devices, synthesizer implementations can range from simple to complex. An inexpensive synthesizer, designed mostly as a stand-alone unit, may have as basic a MIDI implementation as note on/off . . . period. On the other hand, expander modules tend to be quite flexible (assignable controller numbers and the like) since they are designed to work with a wide range of master keyboards. Multitimbral synthesizers provide the advantage of being able to assign each voice to its own channel (an important feature when working with MIDI sequencers).

If the synthesizer has an arpeggiator or built-in sequencer, you may be able to start and stop the sequencer via MIDI, as well as sync it to MIDI timing messages. However, in other cases the manufacturer might not design the sequencer to sync to MIDI timing. The rationale would be that if you have a more powerful sequencer you wouldn't use the on-board sequencer anyway, and if you don't have another sequencer then the on-board one will always be the master. These are some of the reasons why you need to read specification sheets carefully and make sure you ask plenty of questions before buying a piece of gear.

Typical Product: Casio CZ-101

The CZ-101 is a small, inexpensive minikeyboard that nonetheless offers a staggering variety of programming options. As such, it is not only a useful instrument by itself but makes an excellent MIDI expander.

This eight-voice instrument (four-voice for the many programs that use doubled sounds) transmits and receives over any of the available 16 MIDI channels in Poly or Mono mode (Omni on/off messages are ignored). In Mono mode the CZ-101 can provide up to four independent melody lines, with different timbres, assigned to four different MIDI channels; after selecting the basic MIDI channel, the remaining three voices are automatically assigned to the next three higher-numbered MIDI channels.

The CZ-101 has three types of program memory: 16 preset programs (these can be edited but not stored in their edited form), 16 internal programs (these can be altered and stored in their edited form), and 16 external cartridge programs (the cartridge may be blank and store additional user programs or include preloaded programs).

Velocity and aftertouch are neither sent nor received. Available controllers include pitch bend, vibrato on/off (controller number 1), portamento time (controller number 5), master tune (controller number 6), and portamento on/off (controller number 65). The latter two controllers receive data only; the CZ-101 does not transmit master tune or portamento on/off data. **Program select** messages can be transmitted and received, or ignored if the **program select** function is disabled.

As an example of how **program change** works, consider an Akai AX-80 transmitting to the CZ-101. The AX-80 programs are also organized as three banks: Preset (editable but not storable in their edited form) plus two additional banks (A & B) of internal programs which may be edited and stored in their edited form. However, the AX-80 provides 32 programs per bank instead of the Casio's 16. As you would expect, calling up Preset 1 on the AX-80 calls up Preset 1 on the CZ-101, and so on down to Preset 16. Calling up Preset 17 on the AX-80 "rolls over" the Casio back to Preset 1, so selecting Akai Preset 18 calls up Casio Preset 2, Akai Preset 19 calls up Casio Preset 3, and so on until selecting Preset 32 on the AX-80 calls up Casio Preset 16. Selecting programs from Bank A on the AX-80 calls up the CZ-101's Internal programs (1 through 16) in a similar manner, and I assume calling up programs from Bank B of the AX-80 would have called up cartridge programs 1 through 16 except that the CZ-101 I was testing didn't have a RAM cartridge.

Since there are no rhythmic aspects to the CZ-101 (i.e., sequencer or arpeggiator),

no system clock commands are implemented. This instrument also ignores any song-related, **reset**, **active sensing**, and **all notes off** messages but does receive local control on/off messages. Finally, like many other instruments a **system exclusive** function allows for transferring all memory data via MIDI. The next chapter tells how this feature can be used, in conjunction with a home computer and proper accessory software, to create patch libraries.

Typical Product: Yamaha DX-7

The DX-7 is one of the most popular keyboards ever made and not without good reason. Thanks to a sound generation system that is different from most synthesizers, it provides synthesists with a new type of tonal resource—and does so in a compact package at a relatively low price.

Concerning MIDI, the main drawback of the DX-7 is that it works in Omni mode only and transmits exclusively on channel 1 (although it can receive on any of the 16 MIDI channels). Therefore, using the DX-7 to program a non-Yamaha multitrack sequencer can be frustrating, since it is not possible to send data to the sequencer over MIDI channels 2 through 16; however, this limitation can be easily overcome with the right accessory (see Chapter 8). Another problem is the lack of local on/off, which is too bad—the DX-7 would make a perfect master keyboard/expander combo for a sequencer-based MIDI setup. For what it's worth, Yamaha is rumored to be coming out with a software update that fixes the transmit channel limitation.

The DX-7 transmits and receives the following information: note on/off, pitch bend, **program change**, modulation (wheel, aftertouch, breath controller, velocity, etc.), and sustain on/off. A **system exclusive** mode allows for loading and saving all the programmable memory data. Many software developers have taken advantage of this feature to create library and "utility" programs that make the DX-7 easier to use and program (for example, Yamaha's CX5M computer runs several DX-7 related programs). Assuming you want a wide choice of sounds for your instrument, loading programs from library disks is much cheaper in the long run than buying the DX-7 plug-in memory cartridges.

Pitch (Voice, Guitar, Woodwind, etc.) to MIDI Converters

There are a growing number of devices that convert an acoustic instrument's signal to MIDI. Some of these are monophonic and designed for tracking voice, wind instruments (MIDI saxophones, anyone?), and other monophonic sound sources. Polyphonic models are usually designed for guitar, as many guitarists would like to be able to interface their axe to MIDI gear.

Pitch-to-MIDI converters have to work hard—it's not easy to extract a signal, decide what pitch it is, and produce a MIDI output. This is especially true with instruments having complex waveforms (guitar, bass) that defy easy translation into MIDI. Most converters have an inherent delay of at least 20 milliseconds, which is very noticeable unless you're triggering programs with long attack times (swelling string chords, for example).

All of these converters are, at present, relatively limited in the amount of MIDI information they transmit. One important limitation of low-cost converters is that MIDI note data is quantized into half-step intervals—so if you bend a string three half-steps sharp, instead of gliding smoothly the pitch will jump between each step. Some electronic guitars circumvent this problem by including an all-electronic *vibrato tailpiece*, which feels and looks like a standard guitar vibrato tailpiece but is electrically the same as a synthesizer pitch bend wheel.

Despite these present limitations, instrument-to-MIDI converters provide a way for vocalists and many other musicians to orchestrate entire compositions via MIDI sequencing (see Chapter 7). Besides, musical engineers are inventive types, and most of the problems involved with pitch-to-MIDI conversion will probably be solved before too long.

Typical Product: IVL Pitchrider

The Pitchrider has an external input, typically used with a microphone, to pick up an instrument's sound. Although originally de-signed as a pitch detection device to help students learn if they were singing or playing on pitch (as indicated by a readout), the addition of a MIDI output makes the device useful for wind instrument players and vocalists who want to interface to MIDI instruments. The Pitchrider transmits note on/off, pitch bend, velocity, and aftertouch (level) information, with the latter derived from the player's dynamics. The Pitchrider is also available as a plug-in cartridge for the Commodore 64 computer, which provides the same functions as the standard Pitchrider at less than half the cost (see **Fig. 5-3**).

IVL has also developed the rack-mount, six-channel Pitchrider 7000 (**Fig. 5-4**). Attaching IVL's hex pickup to a guitar (so that each string can feed its own pitch-to-MIDI converter) produces a guitar-to-MIDI converter. One particularly interesting feature is that each string can be assigned to a different MIDI channel, thus giving multitimbral effects.

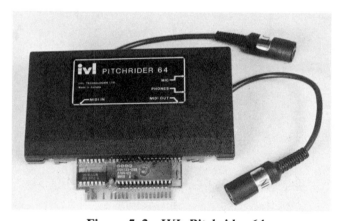

Figure 5-3. *IVL Pitchrider 64*

Figure 5-4. *Pitchrider 7000*

Typical Product: Roland GR-700

The GR-700 was the first workable MIDI guitar synthesizer. Although it is not multitimbral, it covers the note range of 36-96 and transmits both program change and velocity information. All MIDI data is transmitted over channel 1 (other channels cannot be selected).

Although the GR-700 includes a fairly complete synthesizer, it does not have a MIDI input. Therefore, the sound-generating electronics cannot be used as an expander for other MIDI instruments.

Electronic Guitar Controllers

SynthAxe and Octave-Plateau (OP) have both developed MIDI guitar controllers that are based on different principles from pitch-to-voltage converters. The main advantage is speed; the OP MIDI guitar typically processes a new pitch, complete with velocity information, in about half a millisecond. Both the SynthAxe and OP guitars provide full access to the resources of an attached MIDI synthesizer.

The OP guitar has bipolar pitchbending—bend up to raise pitch, bend down to lower pitch. The bend signal may be optionally routed to any MIDI controller. There are two "pressure plates," which may be assigned to any MIDI controllers (typically vibrato, portamento, filter cutoff, and so on). There are also some assignable rotary controls. All this is controlled by a 16-key keypad, eight-digit alphanumeric LED display, and four quick-access buttons. It can transmit either in Poly mode (one channel for all six strings) or in Mono mode (one channel per string). Mono mode provides much more satisfactory guitar-type articulation (independent pitch bends and finger vibrato, for example) and also allows separate programs per string for live orchestration effects. Unfortunately, most current synths respond only in Poly mode, and some that claim Mono operation doesn't have separate pitch bend for each voice.

The SynthAxe has similarly flexible control routings but also provides pressure-sensitive keys for articulation, thus allowing new kinds of expression.

Electronic Drum Pad Controllers

We'll cover drum machines shortly. For now, let's consider MIDI drum pads, as popularized by Simmons. These pads, when struck, trigger the voices in MIDI synthesizers and send velocity information to control dynamics. Thus, synthesizer sounds can double any existing drum sound for intricate, layered effects. Generally each pad can be assigned to its own channel; or all pads can be assigned to one channel, with each pad hitting a different note from the MIDI slave instrument. Usually different programs of drum sounds and channel assignments can be stored and recalled via MIDI **program change** controls.

Dynamic drum pads also allow a drummer to record MIDI drum information into a sequencer. On playback the sequencer can feed MIDI synthesizers (or drum synthesizers with MIDI inputs) and thus reproduce the drum part. Many drummers use this technique to program repetitive parts into a sequencer. On playback they then play fills along with the programmed parts.

Typical Product: Simmons MTM

The MTM is an add-on to the Simmons SDS7 electronic drum kit and enables the latter to transmit and receive MIDI information. Each pad can be assigned to its own MIDI channel. Other features include a MIDI echo function (where MIDI information is delayed and then used to retrigger a drum sound), arpeggiation, programmable dynamics for matching the drum pad dynamics to your own playing style, *dynamic response chords* (where hitting a pad harder plays more notes from a chord), and an interface so that acoustic drums or drum sounds on tape can trigger either the SDS7 or other MIDI instruments.

Drum Machines

Drum machines, being such rhythmic devices, are mostly interested in MIDI timing information. More complete implementations also respond to **song select** and **song pointer** data, which can be invaluable when using the drums in conjunction with a sequencer. As mentioned earlier in the book, **song pointer** data allows for starting drum machines and sequencers at any point in a sequence—for example, if you tell the drums (which act as the master) to start at measure 48, the sequencer will position itself at the beginning of measure 48. Upon pressing the drum's **start** button, both units will start playing at measure 48; and they will remain in sync throughout the composition providing that they are both synced to a common clock.

Another use for MIDI is to program drum dynamics. It's expensive to build velocity-sensitive buttons on a drum machine, so most manufacturers just include a simple on/off switch to trigger drum sounds. But it's not expensive to allow the drums to respond to velocity (dynamics) information appearing at the MIDI In jack. Therefore, if you plug a velocity-sensitive keyboard into the drum's MIDI In, playing individual keyboard keys will trigger individual drum sounds with full dynamics. If you trigger drums from a velocity keyboard while programming a drum pattern, the velocity information will usually be recorded along with the pattern. Note that you aren't limited to using a velocity keyboard—many electronic drum pads also send out velocity data, which makes them ideal for programming rhythm units. Sequencers can also be used, providing precise visual editing of drum patterns, complete control over dynamics, greatly expanded memory, and other advantages. However, sequencers do not offer some popular drum unit functions such as swing and other "humanizing" effects.

Although different machines "map" (assign) different drums to different MIDI notes, the following mapping is used by at least a few manufacturers (including Sequential and E-mu). Some other drum machines, such as Yamaha's RX-11 and RX-15, have assignable drums which can be mapped to any desired MIDI note.

35   Bass drum
36   Rim shot
37   Bass drum
38   Snare drum
39   Handclap
40   Snare drum
41   Low tom
42   Closed hi hat
43   Low tom
44   Closed hi hat
45   Mid tom
46   Open hi hat
47   Mid tom
48   High tom

49   Crash cymbal
50   High tom
51   Ride cymbal
54   Tambourine
56   Cowbell
58   Cabasa

Typical Products: Sequential Drumtraks and Tom

The Drumtraks was one of the first MIDI drum machines. Thanks to MIDI, interfacing two Drumtraks allows for some special functions; for example, pressing **start** on the master will only cause the slave to start *if* it is in song mode. Also, when the slave receives the **start** command it automatically knows to use the MIDI clock input as a timing reference instead of its internal clock. As you might expect, stopping the master also stops the slave. You can additionally select the MIDI channel (1 to 16), whether note (drum) on/off messages are sent from the master to the slave, the mode (Omni on/Poly or Omni off/Poly), and **song select** (selecting a song on the master calls up the corresponding song on the slave). Multiple Drumtraks can transfer data between each other using **system exclusive** messages.

Tom, a newer drum machine from Sequential (**Fig. 5-5**), includes fairly esoteric MIDI features, such as controlling drum tuning, panning, and level via a MIDI keyboard's pitch wheels. Incidentally, SCI is very good about MIDI documentation; separate MIDI Guides, which describe the MIDI options in some detail, are available for most of their products.

Figure 5-5. *Sequential Tom*

Typical Product: E-mu Drumulator retrofit

The Drumulator was introduced prior to the widespread acceptance of MIDI, but eventually a MIDI retrofit became available. Since the Drumulator was not designed with MIDI in mind, the MIDI interface doesn't do much. However, I selected this as a typical product since it illustrates some of the compromises involved in trying to adapt non-MIDI gear to the MIDI spec.

Setting the reception channel (1 to 16) is the first step in entering the Drumulator's MIDI mode. *All* Drumulator functions then become inoperative, except that the drum sounds can now be played dynamically from a velocity MIDI keyboard (the non-MIDI model does not allow for dynamics). Therefore, sequencer tracks programmed from a velocity-sensitive keyboard can play back the velocity and note data into the Drumulator to provide a rhythm pattern with dynamic response. Remember, though, that in MIDI mode the Drumulator becomes a sound-generating device only, which means you're throwing away a lot of its capabilities for the privilege of programming dynamic drum parts via a sequencer.

MIDI Minisequencers

We will cover full-fledged, computer-based, multitrack MIDI sequencers in the next chapter. However, there are now several minisequencers available, and these serve as a good introduction to MIDI recording.

Prior to MIDI many musicians built up multiple tracks of sound by using a two-track tape recorder to "bounce" tracks from one channel to another. For example, you could record a drum track in the right channel, then take the right channel output, mix in some bass (which you would play while listening to the drum track), and record the composite signal in the left channel. The next step would be to bounce the left channel audio, plus another "live" track, into the right channel. The main problem is that since you are premixing each track, the level has to be just right—once you have combined, say, bass and drums on one track, there's no way to go back and change the drum level if you later decide it's not right. There are other limas well: the more times you bounce, the

more noise and distortion accumulates, until the sound quality turns to . . . well, something unpleasant.

Two-track minisequencers (four-track types are also available) serve an analogous purpose. However, unlike a tape recorder, noise and distortion are not problems since you're bouncing *data* between tracks instead of the actual sounds. By recording parts that are "stamped" with different channel information, on playback the MIDI output can drive multiple instruments; each instrument can have its own volume setting in order to obtain the proper mix. Best of all, editing is easier, more efficient, and far more precise than with a tape recorder.

Once you create a sequence, the question then becomes how to save it. Some sequencers have built-in disk drives; others offer a cassette interface; and still others let you dump the information via MIDI to a personal computer. Interestingly, the data dump format used by the Yamaha QX7 two-track sequencer and QX1 eight-track sequencer is identical, so parts worked out on the smaller sequencer can be transferred rapidly over to its "big brother." For bands that use a QX1, each band member could own the much less expensive QX7 for working out individual parts and this data could then be loaded into the QX1 during rehearsals.

Of course, similarity of data format is not a necessity to transfer parts from one sequencer to another. As long as one unit can output a MIDI clock and the other can sync to it, you can move data between sequencers just by playing data from the master's MIDI Out into the slave's MIDI In. This technique is very handy for live performance—work out complex sequences at home on a fancy computer, then transfer these parts to inexpensive minisequencers for live use so you don't have to drag your computer around with you. However, don't attempt to speed up the transfer process by drastically increasing the tempo because timing errors might result.

For the full story on MIDI sequencers, see Chapter 7.

Typical Product: Korg SQD-1

The SQD-1 (See **Fig. 5-6**) is a remarkably complete two-track, 16-channel sequencer,

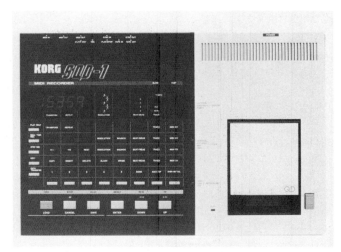

Figure 5-6. *Korg SQD-1 minisequencer*

complete with a Quick Disk for saving sequence data. The Quick Disk is a member of the floppy-disk family but is smaller than the 5¼″ and 8″ disks used with most personal computers. Unlike regular floppy disks, which can instantly access any part of the disk, a Quick Disk starts reading data at the beginning of a disk and reads all the way through to the end. A good analogy would be operating a record turntable. Normally, to play one song you would set the tonearm down at the beginning of that song and begin listening; similarly, a standard floppy disk can play any "track" on the disk. If the record turntable worked in the same way as a Quick Disk, you would need to play through the entire record in order to hear one specific cut. However, Quick Disks offer enough advantages that you're likely to forgive them for being a little slower than the more costly standard disks. Quick Disks can store a lot of data (about 30,000 notes on both sides of the disk with the SQD-1), and the maximum time needed to transfer a complete song to and from the disk is less than 8 seconds. On the negative side, they seem to be rather fragile . . . so be careful.

In addition to handling note-on/note-off data, the SQD-1 can record and play back on all 16 MIDI channels and do bouncing between tracks. Each channel can have its own part with individual velocity, aftertouch, **program change**, pitch bend, and modulation wheel change. However, since this type of control information eats up a lot of memory, several "filter" switches on the back panel allow the sequencer to ignore certain types of MIDI data. (For example, ignoring after-

touch messages saves a fair amount of memory.) As you might expect, when building up lots of notes, on lots of channels, with lots of modulation information, some timing delays are possible; but overall the response is pretty good.

Once the part is recorded, you have several available editing options—including **copy** (copy a measure to the end of the song), **insert** (insert new measures between already recorded measures), **delete** (remove measures of data), **blank** (erase the contents of a particular measure or measures), **erase** (erase all note data from the end of the specified measure to the end of the song), and, naturally, **punch-in** and **punch-out**. You cannot, however, edit individual notes.

The SQD-1 can synchronize to MIDI clocks as well as external clock pulses, and it includes sync-to-tape. A number of convenience features (fast forward and rewind keys, step-time or real-time recording modes, and so on) make this an unusually versatile low-cost sequencer.

Signal Processors

It used to be that tweaking up signal processor settings was a real drag. If you wanted to change a delay line from, say, flanging to echo, you would often have to flick a couple of switches and twist a couple of controls.

Then came the programmable delay, which stores particular effects in particular memory locations. For example, location number 1 might store a flanging sound; number 2, light chorusing; number 3, heavy chorusing; number 4, doubling; number 5, echo; and so on. Instead of having to fool with several controls to change sounds, you need only select the correct program number.

Now MIDI will change those programs automatically for you, providing that the delay (or other MIDI-controlled signal processor, such as reverb) is receiving MIDI information from a device (sequencer, master keyboard, etc.) that transmits **program select** commands. Let's describe how this would work with a delay line. A song might open with a synthesizer playing an electric piano part, which would require a little chorusing. Upon changing programs to a percussive clavinet part, the delay could react to this program change and give you, say, a tight doubling effect. Finally, as you change programs for a featured solo at the end of the song, the delay line can follow along and give long, spacey echoes.

As with master/slave synth setups, it is your responsibility to make sure that the delay selects the proper effect when it receives a **program change** command—note which delay programs are called up when you select a particular synth program, and program your delay line accordingly.

To change programs at the signal processor without changing the synthesizer program, simply copy the synth program into another program with a different number. Selecting the new program will change sounds on the signal processor; but because the new program contains the same patch data as the previously selected program, the synth sound will remain essentially the same.

Guitarists can also take advantage of MIDI signal processors. For those guitarists who are playing along with a sequencer, the sequencer itself can send out **program change** commands to the signal processor. Otherwise, Peavey makes an accessory MIDI footswitch that allows guitarists to transmit up to 10 different program numbers over MIDI by pressing various footswitches.

Typical Product: Peavey Programmable Effects Processor

The PEP is a delay line that stores 10 different delay programs. These can be recalled via front panel switches or MIDI **program change** commands—which can come from a keyboard, sequencer, or Peavey's RMC 2000 remote MIDI controller footswitch. The PEP can be set to channels 1 through 8 and includes a MIDI Thru jack for when the PEP is used with another PEP or other MIDI effect.

Typical Product: Korg SDD-2000 MIDI Sampling Delay

The SDD-2000 delay line provides slightly over 1 second of delay at 18 kHz bandwidth and slightly over 4 seconds at a reduced 4.5 kHz reduced bandwidth. It provides all standard delay effects and contains 64 different program memories. This allows a synth

with 64 or fewer programs to have a different DDL setting for each synth program, which is selected automatically over MIDI whenever you change programs on the synth.

The SDD also provides several sampling and sequencing modes. The most powerful one allows any sound to be recorded into the SDD memory and then transposed by a MIDI keyboard. Sounds up to 1 second long can be played back over a one-octave range and respond to velocity and pitch wheel messages issued by the MIDI keyboard. Sounds up to 4 seconds may be recorded at reduced bandwidth and played back over a three-octave range. There are special provisions for tuning the sound and selecting the range to be played. Korg supports the SDD with a cassette of 50 sounds and in a range of octaves—but you'll get better fidelity by sampling a live source or Compact Disc.

Recording begins when built-in trigger circuitry detects the initial attack of the sound. The end of the recorded sample can be "trimmed" with a rotary control. Concerning limitations, there are no sampling goodies like reversal or looping; and the SDD is not polyphonic—only one note may be played at a time. Still, this is a useful and cost-effective piece of gear.

MIDI Guitar Amplifiers

It had to happen . . . even guitar amps are MIDIfied. Most amps have footswitches to select between "clean" and "dirty" sounds; but that's about it. To change EQ, reverb, or any other amp parameter, you have to go grab a knob. A MIDI guitar amp stores programs of control settings and accesses each program with **program change** commands. As with signal processors, these **program change** commands can come from a keyboard, sequencer, or MIDI footswitch controller.

Typical Product: Peavey Programax 10

The Programax 10 (**Fig. 5-7**) is a 210-watt RMS (into 4 ohms) guitar amplifier featuring Peavey's "saturation" overdrive circuitry, equalization, and effects loop. Virtually all of the amp parameters can be stored and then recalled, either from the amp front panel or via MIDI **program change** commands.

Mixers

So far, very few MIDI mixers are available. However, that situation will probably change by the time this book comes out.

A basic MIDI mixer simply stores control settings as a program. These programs can later be recalled via MIDI **program change** commands. The advantage of this type of mixer is rapid switching from one mix setup to another. For example, suppose you have a song where the instrument levels change every time you go into a verse, chorus, or instrumental. With a programmable mixer, the mix for each section can be stored as a separate program and recalled when appropriate.

Eventually, faders, EQ in/out, reverb, and so on might be accessible as MIDI controllers. This would allow for true automated mixdown where parameters are changed smoothly, rather than in series of steps (or "snapshots") as described above.

Figure 5-7. *Peavey Programax 10*

Chapter 6

MIDI Applications

So now you know what MIDI is and how it works . . . let's find out what you can do with it.

Multiple Keyboard Control

It's no fun being stuck behind a stack of synthesizers, and MIDI provides a solution. Suppose you have three MIDI synthesizers—two of which (Synthesizers A and B) have MIDI In/Out/Thru jacks and a third (Synth C) which has MIDI In/Out only. Let's also suppose that you want to control synthesizers A, B, and C from a remote master keyboard or similar MIDI-producing device (guitar-to-MIDI interface, wind-instrument-to-MIDI interface, etc.) that includes a single MIDI Out.

Fig. 6-1 shows one possible interconnection scheme. The remote's MIDI Out goes to Synth A's MIDI In. Synth A's MIDI Thru, which provides a replica of the data present at its MIDI In jack, patches to Synth B's MIDI In. Synth B's MIDI Thru would similarly patch to Synth C's MIDI In.

The next step after patching is to determine how the slave synths will respond to the remote master. With all four synths in Omni On mode, the three slave synthesizers will follow whatever you play on the remote. To change programs (patches), check that Synths A, B, and C are set to accept **program change** information (consult their respective manuals for how to do this). When set this way, select-

ing a different program number at the remote would cause a corresponding program change at the other three synthesizers. (Remember—it is up to you to make sure that these programs are sonically compatible. If you want Synth A to play a violin patch, Synth B a cello patch, and Synth C a trumpet line when you select program 1 on the remote, then you must make sure that these particular programs are in the memory locations that are called up when the remote sends out the **program** 1 command.)

So much for program changes . . . but what if you *don't* want all three slave synthesizers playing at once? Simple—create a *null program* (by turning off the synth's VCA, disabling the VCOs, or closing down the filter all the way), and select this null program when you want the synth to be quiet.

Then again, you might want to play *one* synth at a time from the remote. To do this, set each slave for a different channel, and initialize all three to **Omni On**. At first, they will all play together. To play one at a time, send out **Omni Off** commands to all three on their respective channels, and set the remote master to the channel for the slave you want to play. An advanced remote/master with a reasonably complete MIDI implementation might let you program "steps" containing combinations of channel selections, zones (as in the case of the Oberheim Xk), automatic transmissions of **Omni Off** commands when required, and so on . . . otherwise, you'd have

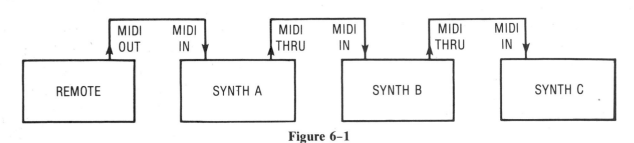

Figure 6-1

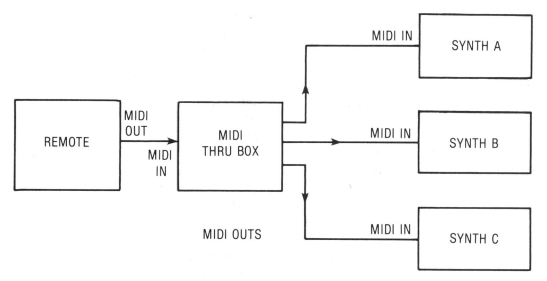

Figure 6-2

to reach over and manually switch modes on all three synths. A switcher/patchbay would probably be an easier alternative, or three MIDI on/off switches (see Chapter 8) could also be used to selectively send MIDI information to one of three slave synthesizers.

There are two possible problems you might encounter with this hookup. The first is that not all synthesizers have MIDI Thru connectors. The second is that it takes a finite amount of time for the MIDI signal to pass through each synthesizer; therefore, the greater the number of synthesizers in the chain, the greater the risk of MIDI data distortion. The solution for either problem is a MIDI Thru (*splitter*) box, which buffers the signal coming from the remote and splits it into individual MIDI outputs for each synth. **Fig. 6-2** shows how you would add a MIDI Thru box to the above-mentioned system.

Drum Machine Setups

Drum machine MIDI implementations are not as standardized as keyboard implementations, so you may have to work a bit harder to integrate a drum machine into your setup. One popular MIDI drum application is to use the dynamics data from a MIDI velocity keyboard to program drum dynamics. (Adding MIDI to a drum machine and programming dynamics via a keyboard is less expensive than designing in velocity-sensitive buttons a la Linn 9000 or E-mu SP-12.) **Fig. 6-3** shows the basic hookup; when program-

ming a drum pattern, instead of hitting the drum unit's nondynamic buttons you would hit the corresponding keys on a MIDI velocity keyboard. Drums that allow for this option will include a chart that indicates which drum sounds are played from which keyboard keys (as mentioned previously in Chapter 5). Note, however, that when some drum machines are set to receive MIDI information, they do not necessarily *record* those notes in memory—in other words, the drum becomes a "playback-only" device.

Another application is to synchronize different MIDI drum machines from different manufacturers together, thus producing fatter, bigger drum sounds than a single device could by itself. Again, though, problems can crop up. Various drum machines take different amounts of time to respond to MIDI data or external clock signals, which means that one drum machine might lag or lead another drum machine connected to the same synchronizing signal. There are several solutions for this problem (time offset boxes, adapters, delays, etc.); however, these tend to be costly.

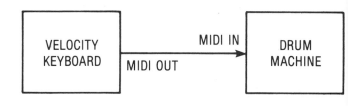

Figure 6-3

Preprogrammed Effects Changes

Changing signal processor settings onstage has always been problematic since tweaking the controls to produce just the right sound can be time-consuming. To partially solve this problem, several manufacturers now make programmable effects devices that memorize several sounds' worth of control settings. Usually the factory supplies an initial selection of sounds, but you are free to modify them as required.

Although programmable units are a big improvement over nonprogrammables with respect to convenience, there are still some problems to be overcome (especially for guitarists, who have both hands occupied when playing). While individual effects can almost always be bypassed via a footswitch, switching more than one piece of gear at a time requires some fancy footwork; and unfortunately, there are many occasions where you will want to switch more than one effect—for example, from straight guitar, to compression-plus-fuzz-plus-echo, then back to straight guitar. (Some multiple effects systems let you set up combinations of effects in advance, whereupon pressing a single master bypass switch brings all preselected effects in, or out, at once. However, these tend to be closed systems where you cannot mix effects from a variety of manufacturers.)

MIDI-compatible special effects devices that react to **program change** commands solve these and other problems. If the musician plays along with a sequencer, the program settings can be changed automatically

by recording **program change** messages on one of the sequencer's tracks. For greater spontaneity a MIDI **program select** footswitch (as made by Peavey; see Chapter 5) lets you push a footswitch to send a **program select** command. For example, a MIDI footswitch might have five footswitches and a **bank select A/B** footswitch. With the **bank select** switch in the A position, the five footswitches would select MIDI program numbers 1 through 5. With the **bank select** switch in the B position, the five footswitches would select MIDI program numbers 6 through 10.

When daisy-chaining signal processors together, sending a **program select** message can change control settings on several signal processors simultaneously (see **Fig. 6-4**). MIDI-compatible mixers open up further possibilities for special effects setups, such as programmable parallel connections of special effects.

Voice Editing Software

In the early days of electronic music, synthesizers had lots of knobs and switches; and each one altered some aspect of the instrument's sound. For example, if you wanted to adjust the filter parameters, there were separate knobs for filter cutoff frequency, resonance, amount of envelope depth, and the like.

But knobs and switches cost money, so engineers designed the *parameter control* synthesizer to make instruments more affordable. This type of instrument numbers each available parameter (filter cutoff, resonance,

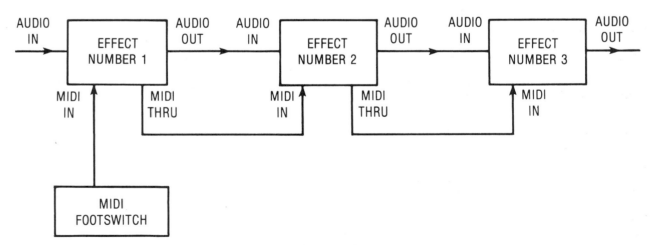

Figure 6-4

envelope attack time, etc.) and uses a calculator-type keypad to specify the number of the parameter you want to change (edit). A single potentiometer then varies the parameter; upon selecting a new parameter, the setting for the previously selected parameter is stored in memory. So, if you want to change a couple of parameters on one of these synthesizers, here's what you would do:

1. Specify the parameter to be changed with the keypad.
2. Adjust the pot to change the parameter value.
3. Specify the next parameter you want to change with the keypad.
4. Adjust the pot to change the parameter value.

This process is more time-consuming than simply grabbing a couple of knobs, but the advantage is low cost—after all, a single pot and calculator keypad costs a whole lot less than multiple controls.

Then manufacturers figured out how to get rid of the pot altogether by using the numeric keypad to specify *values* as well as parameters. With this design, steps 2 and 4 above would read, Specify the parameter value with the keypad. For example, filter cutoff values might range from 00 to 63. Typing in 63 would give a high cutoff frequency, while typing 00 would give a low cutoff frequency.

Although parameter control made the under $1,000 synthesizer a reality, programming some of these machines can be so tedious that many musicians stopped programming altogether and instead bought "canned" sounds programmed by various synthesizer pros.

Voice-editing software makes it much easier to adjust a synthesizer's parameters. Typically, the computer's monitor screen will show the equivalent of the instrument's front panel, with all (or at least most) of the parameter values indicated. Thus, you know at a glance whether you're not hearing the LFO because you turned it off, or didn't route it to the right place, or set the speed too slow for any modulation to be noticeable.

Other programs translate parameter values into something more meaningful to the musician. For example, many synthesizers let you generate multistage envelopes; but all the parameters are invariably expressed numerically, which makes it difficult to visualize the actual shape of the envelope. With the proper software, the envelope shape can be displayed on the monitor to give immediate visual feedback to your editing.

As you might expect, there are many varieties of voice-editing software. Programs are currently available for the DX-7, CZ-101, Mirage, Emulator II, and others. The point here is not to describe exactly what's available but to emphasize that this type of software can be extremely useful if you want to get the most out of your instrument—and not drive yourself crazy with tedium during the programming process. After all, the ability to program your instrument for your own sounds is what will distinguish you as an individual and set you apart from other musicians. It therefore makes good sense to render the programming process as painless as possible.

Patch Library Software

Let's suppose you have created some really great programs for your instrument but have used up all the instrument's memory in the process. Before creating any new programs, you naturally want to save the patch data already in memory. Most instruments have cassette interfaces; and if you're careful (use digital data tape only, set levels properly, maintain your deck, and so on), cassette storage can be a reliable and economical way to store patch data. However, saving and loading data with cassettes can take as much as several minutes, which is a serious problem for live performance.

Some synthesizers circumvent the slow access time of cassettes by storing sounds in external RAM cartridges. Unfortunately, these tend to be rather pricey, and saving 10 complete banks of sounds could cost anywhere from $500 to $1000. Probably the best option is to save patch data on floppy disks, which are inexpensive ($2-$5 each) and hold vast quantities of digital data. Disk drives are relatively costly, so you're not going to find them built into every musical instruments; fortunately, though, most personal computers already have disk drives. So, all that's needed is some way to translate the instrument patch data into digital information that can be fed into the computer, then stored on floppy disks.

The answer? As you might recall from Chapter 4, many manufacturers use **system exclusive** messages to transfer patch data (via MIDI) from one synthesizer to another synthesizer of the same make and model. There's no reason why this patch data can't be sent to a computer instead of another instrument, stored on a floppy disk, and reloaded from the computer back into the instrument as needed.

Many of these *sound filing* or *patch library* software programs provide some bonus features, such as being able to name programs once they're in the computer. Thus, if you want to recall that great laser-blaster sound effect, you simply specify the "Laser Blaster" program instead of having to remember a patch number.

Although saving and loading to disk is convenient, don't forget about the rigors of the road: toting around inexpensive home computers and disk drives, which are not necessarily built to rock and roll specs, can mean frequent breakdowns. So, treat the equipment carefully, build a flight case, and if possible, keep a spare computer and disk drive available at all times. And back up your disks! It's a true catastrophe when someone spills a glass of water on the disk that took you months of work to tweak to perfection. For maximum security while on the road, take a set of backups with you but also keep a set at home.

Data Transfer

Although many machines can save their data on cassette, disk, or cartridge, it is far more difficult to transfer data between *different* machines, especially models from different manufacturers. Sound data is virtually impossible to transfer; but sequencer information can often be exchanged from one device to another, and so can some drum parts.

When transferring parts from one sequencer to another, the trick is to sync the two devices together so that they are running from a common clock. Typically, the sequencer containing the part to be transmitted

will be the master, and the one receiving the data will be the slave. Assuming that starting the master also starts the slave at the same time, hook the master's MIDI output(s) to the slave's MIDI input(s), select the master track to be transferred, put the slave in **record** mode for that track, press **start**; and the track will play from the master into the slave. Usually you will have to transfer one track (or MIDI channel) at a time, although some sequencers have multiple inputs and outputs. If the slave has less memory available than the master, you may be able to filter out memory-hungry data from the MIDI data stream (i.e., aftertouch data) in order to use up less of the slave's memory.

This transfer technique can sometimes be used within a *single* sequencer to modify a track. Suppose a track has been recorded in real-time on sequencer track 1. On playback the sequencer's MIDI Out can be patched to the MIDI In, and track 1 bounced over to a different track which is set for a particular rhythmic quantization. You could then decide whether you liked the quantized or non-quantized track better and erase the one which is no longer needed.

As of this writing, there is a definite movement towards creating a common-file data transfer format for the Roland MPU-401 computer interface. Various people in the industry are working on this, and although there are certain problems—such as corporate politics—the idea is a good one and hopefully something will come of it. The idea is *not* that everyone will use the same data format, since different sequencer design goals require different internal data structures. Rather, the intent is to have a common format to which everyone can read and write, so that songs can be moved between sequencers. Each manufacturer would then offer a program to translate their files to this common format.

Since the common format will normally be for translation rather than direct playback, people using devices other than the MPU-401 can still use it for translating their (Passport, Syntech, Sequential, or whatever interface) files into something readable by other software—and vice versa. In theory, files created on the Macintosh, Commodore 64, Amiga, Apple IIe, and IBM PC could all talk to each other using this format and could even be exchanged via modems or electronic mail (also see the section in this chapter on "Telecommunications").

Prerecorded MIDI Practice Tracks

Remember the "Music Minus One" records? These were recordings of music without one of the instrumentalists. The idea was that you could play along with the record and supply the missing track to improve your chops. Some software suppliers now offer accessory disks, prerecorded with MIDI musical data, to go along with their MIDI sequencer systems. This is the modern-day equivalent of supplying punched paper rolls for player pianos. As an added bonus, since the music is stored on disk, you can generally edit it, erase tracks, or whatever else suits your fancy.

Telecommunications

The *modem* (short for modulator/demodulator) serves as a computer-to-phone-line/phone-line-to-computer interface. The transmitting computer's modem converts digital data into audio tones that can be sent through the phone lines, received by another computer, and then converted back into digital data by the receiving computer's modem. Telecommunications is great fun: one application is to send electronic mail back and forth between consenting computers; another is to dial up a data base containing information that interests you (news and weather, arts, synthesizer/MIDI fanatics, airline schedules, travel information, and a lot more).

Since MIDI is nothing more than a stream of digital data, it can also be sent through the phone lines via a modem. Yes, the day has finally arrived where you can literally "phone in your part;" but you theoretically can do much more. There is even talk of dial-a-patch services, where you would call up a data base and load patches into your synthesizer over the phone lines. The main problem at this point is incompatibility between programs. As one example, notation files are very difficult to transfer from one program to a different program, which would make it hard for a composer in New York to

---

Transferring Drum Data via Non-MIDI Methods

Transferring drum data between two machines can usually be accomplished without MIDI; however, the transmitting drum machine must have individual drum sound audio outputs and the slave must have individual trigger inputs for its drum sounds. Note that this technique can only transfer segment or pattern information, *not* song information (such as which segments are strung together in what order). Also note that the drum audio outputs will need to be converted into digital triggers capable of driving the receiver's trigger inputs; several commercially available accessories exist for this purpose, or you can use a standard analog synthesizer envelope follower module.

Patch the transmitter's audio outputs to the slave's trigger inputs through the appropriate converter box—bass audio out to bass trigger in, snare audio out to snare trigger in, and so on. Set the slave machine segment length to the same number of measures as the segment being played on the master; set quantization as desired; and make sure the slave is set to accept an external clock input. Synchronize the two drum machines to the same clock, and start them simultaneously. (Starting at the same time can be a problem with non-MIDI machines, although most rhythm units include an external run/stop footswitch jack. You can generally use a Y-cord to send a footswitch output into both run/stop jacks, which lets you start both machines at the same time from a single press of the footswitch.) **Fig. 6-5** summarizes the hookup.

As the drum sounds play from the transmitter, they will trigger the same drum sounds on the receiver, and these triggers will be recorded into the receiver's memory. There may be a slight timing lag between the two drums, but this problem can almost always be compensated for by running the clock very slowly as you transfer the parts and using quantization.

"modem" a lead sheet to an artist in Los Angeles (unless they use the same composing program).

Another problem—which is more readily overcome—is that many modems are set up to transmit and receive only text files, not synthesizer patch data in binary form. However, modems with software capable of supporting the *X-modem* protocol (developed by Ward Christiansen, who rather than trying to make a quick buck off of it, placed it in the public domain) can send and receive nontext

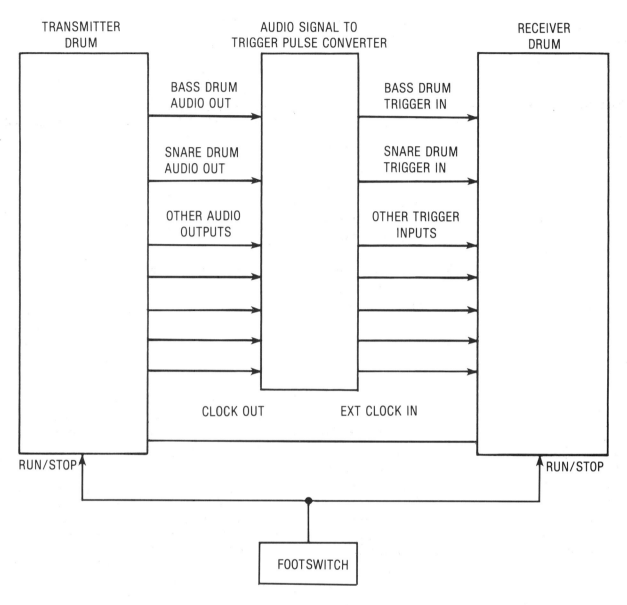

Figure 6–5

files and also perform a considerable amount of error-checking to make sure that all received data matches the transmitted data. Musicians who are considering purchasing a modem are advised to find one that accepts the X-modem protocol.

Lead Sheet Printing

Some sequencers have built-in software for printing lead sheets, but many lead sheet printing programs are designed as accessory programs for existing sequencer or composition software. Music-printing software varies greatly in quality, ease of use, resolution, speed of operation, and MIDI compatibility. Some cannot reproduce certain elementary

functions, such as ties; yet others can produce multipart, high-resolution printouts. Although it will take you a fair amount of research to find the printing software that's right for you, the work is worth it if you want to tell a computer to print out a score instead of having to do the whole thing by hand.

MIDI Echo Units and Arpeggiators

A *MIDI echo unit* (also called a *MIDI digital delay*) receives MIDI data at its MIDI In jack, delays the data, then plays the data back through its MIDI Out jack. (Do not confuse this device with a MIDI-controlled delay line, which is an audio signal processor

Note Graphics versus Non-Note Graphics

Using traditional note graphics is not the only way to go for sequencers; some programs represent notes in nontraditional ways. Some of the disadvantages of using standard note graphics for interacting with a sequencer are as follows:

- Note graphics force you to work at the note level, so if lots of notes are displayed, just getting around the page can be time-consuming.
- Time is required for converting from recorded data to graphics and vice versa after corrections are made. This hinders the tight feedback loop needed for effective composition—you can't instantly switch from **play**, to **edit**, to **play**, to **edit** since you have to wait for the computer to process all the graphic information.
- Note graphics are handy if you're doing scores for studio musicians or creating a lead sheet for copyright purposes. But if these functions are not a major part of your work, make sure that you judge a sequencer on its all-around capabilities, not just on its ability to create pleasing displays.

whose programs are called up via **program change** messages.)

Fig. 6-6 shows how to hook up a MIDI delay to a typical synthesizer. Playing a note on the synthesizer sends note data to the delay; once a settable period of time has elapsed (usually up to 1 second), the data plays back into the keyboard and produces an echo of the original note. (Remember that most of the time MIDI In and MIDI Out are active simultaneously, so the synthesizer will respond to notes played on the keyboard *and* notes received at the MIDI In jack unless local control is off. Of course, the synth cannot play more notes than it has voices available to play those notes.) The big advantage of a MIDI delay is that the echo has *perfect* fidelity, since data, not sound, is being delayed: When used with a single instrument, the echoed note is a product of the same sound-generating circuitry that played the original note.

It is also possible to create multiple repeats by reading the MIDI data out of the delay more than once. By lowering the velocity value each time the data is read, the echo can fade out. However, since each echo requires its own synthesizer voice, multiple echoes quickly use up the available synthesizer voices. Therefore many MIDI delays

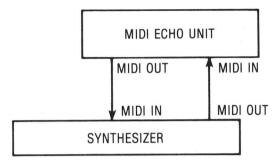

Figure 6-6

offer but a single slapback echo, or perhaps a couple of repeats.

Some delays can even transpose the data up or down an octave, which is a particularly tasty effect—like having a glitchless pitch transposer with perfect fidelity. And you're not restricted to using the delay with a single keyboard; sending the delay to an expander box (**Fig. 6-7**) can give echoes with a radically different timbre from the original note.

MIDI delays are less costly than standard audio digital delay lines. So if you have a tight budget but need echo on both vocals and keyboards, use a standard DDL with non-MIDI tracks (such as vocals) and a MIDI echo unit with keyboards.

MIDI arpeggiators work similarly to MIDI delays. Typically, you enter the arpeggiation parameters (over what range to arpeggiate, the dynamics, whether to arpeggiate up or down, etc.). As you play chords and notes, these will be arpeggiated according the parameters you've entered. As with MIDI delay, the arpeggiator output data could feed an expander box, thus creating arpeggios that sound different from the original notes being played.

The field of MIDI data processing is still in its infancy. Some data processors are stand-alone units, while others are built-in to existing software programs. There's no reason why future products couldn't provide chromatic "harmonization" effects, or diatonic rather than chromatic transposition, or even instant chordal accompaniment to melody lines . . . we'll see what the future brings.

* * * * *

One of the most important MIDI applications is the MIDI recording studio. In fact, this application is so important that it has its very own chapter . . . so read on.

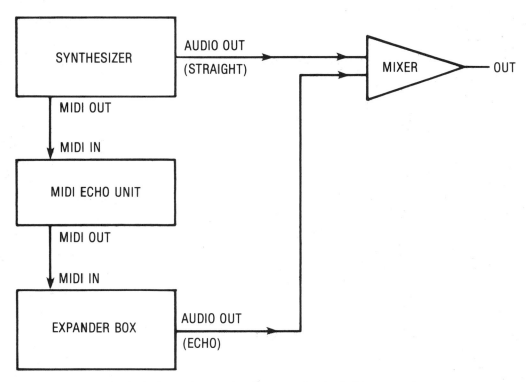

THE ECHO HAS A DIFFERENT TIMBRE FROM THE STRAIGHT SOUND.

Figure 6–7

Chapter 7

The MIDI Studio

This is one of the most important MIDI applications of all. The MIDI sequencer has now made it possible to create an entirely different kind of recording studio for electronic music (whether home or commercial recording). As mentioned previously, when you play a melodic line on a MIDI keyboard, the computer-based sequencer remembers what you play and assigns this data to a track in the sequencer. You can build up multiple tracks and, on playback, send this musical data to multiple MIDI slave instruments—thus producing the same effect as if you had multitracked the instruments with a conventional multitrack tape recorder. The outputs of the instruments being sequenced can then be mixed and recorded onto a conventional two-track analog recorder, digital recorder, or (for maximum fidelity) PCM adapter/VCR combination to produce a master tape. (Some musicians record onto the audio tracks of Beta or VHS Hi-Fi machines, which also offer excellent fidelity.) That's merely a cursory look at the process; before getting into details, let's consider some of the advantages of MIDI recording via sequencer over conventional analog tape recording.

MIDI Studio Advantages and Disadvantages

Some of the advantages are as follows:

- First-generation sound quality. What you hear on your final master is the sound of the MIDI instruments, with no intervening tape processes to degrade their clarity. In a MIDI studio, the multitrack tape recorder is an option, not a necessity.
- No rewind time when working out compositions. Until the final mixdown, everything is stored in computer memory for virtually instant access.

- Zero fidelity loss when bouncing, no matter how many times you bounce. After all, you're bouncing computer data instead of sound.
- The ability to edit as little as one thirty-second note of one instrument on one track. Forget about the problems of such techniques as the "window splice" (where, with tape, you splice a tiny window out of a multitrack tape to eliminate one bad note).
- Dramatically lower tape and maintenance costs. You don't have to align the bias or azimuth of a MIDI sequencer, or oil the motor, or even worry too much about temperature and humidity extremes.
- Instantly change the sound of a track. Would that violin track sound better as a trumpet? Change presets on the instrument being driven from the track and find out; there's no need to do any rerecording.
- No noise reduction needed (unless you want to add some when you mix your multitracked composition over to a master tape).

And to be fair, let's cover the disadvantages as well.

- Tape saturation, which is often used to "warm up" a sound, is not possible.
- You need a separate synthesizer, or separate voice of a multitimbral synthesizer, for each voice you want to play back. With conventional multitrack recording, you can overdub the same synth any number of times; but to play back MIDI tracks, you need some kind of sound-generating device for each and every track you record. Obviously, the cost of this approach adds up pretty rapidly . . . although using one or two polyphonic synths, plus a good multitimbral synth, can handle most of your needs.

- With conventional multitrack recording, one signal processor can be used over and over again for different tracks. With MIDI recording, each track to be processed requires its own signal processor.
- Your mixer must be able to accommodate a large number of inputs.
- A high-powered sequencer, hooked up to a high-power (read: expensive) computer, is necessary for large MIDI setups involving lots of equipment.

Of course, where disadvantages exist, there are ways to get around them. Premixes of several MIDI instruments can be recorded on a single tape track; and by synchronizing the MIDI sequencer to a click track recorded on tape, these same instruments can later play back different parts onto another track in perfect synchronization with the first premix. This reduces the need for multiple sound-generating devices. If you save all the track data for the premixed parts on disk, it's even rather easy to go back and re-do parts, as needed, later on. This approach works best if you don't mix acoustic and electronic instruments when doing premixes.

Although MIDI recording does not replace conventional tape recording (yet), if you were considering upgrading an 8-track recorder to a 16- or 24-track model, you might want to reconsider. MIDI can upgrade your studio to a lot more tracks for a lot less bucks. Using a computerized sequencer to control MIDI instruments is not as expensive as you might think since over the past few years computer memory costs have declined to the point where you can store thousands and thousands of pieces of MIDI data in a very inexpensive computer. In fact, you could easily base an "entry-level" MIDI studio around the Commodore 64, an inexpensive and common machine.

Let's first consider the components that make up a MIDI studio and, then, what is involved with the art of MIDI recording.

Instruments for the MIDI Studio

The first step in creating a MIDI studio is to gather together some MIDI instruments; after all, these are what make the sounds. Your choice of instruments will largely be a matter of taste and budget, but here are some suggestions.

A MIDI sampling keyboard is an expensive but important item. While sequencing all-electronic sounds can be very satisfying, adding in some "real-world" sounds gives you a much broader sonic palette. I've also found that doubling sampled sounds with synthetic sounds usually comes across more forcefully than either sound by itself. Even a relatively inexpensive instrument such as the Ensoniq Mirage (or the Decillionix sampling program hooked up to an Apple II) can do wonders, and naturally a high-tech instrument like the Emulator II or Kurzweil 250 can do proportionately more. Rack-mount samplers (such as Akai's model S612), which can be controlled by any MIDI keyboard, are an economical alternative to buying a full-fledged sampling keyboard instrument, as are digital delays with sampling capabilities (such as the DeltaLab CompuEffectron or Korg SDD-2000).

You will also want some kind of expander sound module. An expander is basically a synthesizer without the keyboard; it is accessed solely via MIDI. Because it doesn't have a keyboard, you can save some bucks compared to a standard keyboard instrument with equivalent capabilities. There are many good expander modules available. Although the following is subject to change in the months ahead as new gear works its way into the marketplace, for now I particularly like the Oberheim Xpander because the MIDI implementation is very complete, because it sounds great, and because it is far more flexible than the average synth. In the low-price category, Casio's CZ-101 minikeyboard makes a fine expander module because it provides good-sounding voices for little cost. Yamaha and Roland make a number of their products available in an expander box format, as does Korg; and some of Sequential's low-cost keyboards (like the Six-Trak and Max) make cost-effective MIDI expanders.

Multitimbral expander boxes and keyboards are particularly useful in a MIDI studio. These instruments can provide a unique timbre (bass, trumpet, violin, etc.) for *each voice* in the synthesizer, as well as assign each voice to its own MIDI channel. Thus, multitimbral instruments such as the Xpander,

Six-Trak, or CZ-101 can give you independent melody lines (one per voice) when driven by a MIDI sequencer. Remember, though, that as we mentioned earlier some multitimbral synths handle pitch bend on a per-voice basis, while others apply pitch bend data globally to all voices . . . check before you buy.

Guitarists, and players of acoustic instruments, are not out of the picture by any means. As described in Chapter 5, several companies make guitar-to-MIDI converters, while simpler monophonic devices let vocalists, wind instrument players, and others program MIDI devices from their instruments. As you might expect, these instrument-to-MIDI converters tend to have less complete MIDI implementations than a MIDI keyboard, since nonelectronic instruments are much harder to adapt to MIDI. Most guitar-to-MIDI converters cannot send pitch bend information over MIDI (they instead quantize all notes in semitone steps) and do not offer Mono mode or much remote control of MIDI synthesizers beyond program changes. Another problem is "processing lag"—the time it takes for a computer to analyze the sound and convert this data to MIDI information.

Still, most of these limitations are well worth working around in order to gain the advantages of interfacing traditional instruments with the MIDI studio. There's something about playing a sampled piano sound from a guitar that is really quite mind-boggling (or at least ear-boggling). Recently introduced controllers designed specifically for MIDI (such as the Octave Plateau and SynthAxe guitar controllers; see Chapter 5) provide a high degree of control over MIDI synthesizers and claim to have a far smaller amount of processing lag. Instruments like these, while expensive, should give guitarists the same degree of freedom and access to MIDI resources that keyboard players have enjoyed all along.

You'll also need a MIDI drum machine—hopefully one which responds to velocity information and song data (i.e., the drum unit automatically switches to the desired song upon command). Fortunately, though, many older non-MIDI drum machines will work with MIDI sequencers that have provisions for sending out a drum-compatible clock pulse signal. Adapters are also available (see Chapter 8) that convert MIDI timing signals into the timing signals used by older drum machines.

The most important point to remember is that, to be most effective in the MIDI studio, any MIDI instrument should have as complete a MIDI implementation as possible. You should at least be able to receive, and preferably transmit, on all 16 channels. Being able to transmit a keyboard's velocity (dynamics) information over MIDI is also very important, because it lets you do your own mix as you play (velocity keyboards are also great for programming MIDI drum units that accept dynamic information). Expander boxes need to be capable of receiving this velocity information and responding to it.

Program change over MIDI, where changing a program on the master also causes a corresponding program change on slave instruments, is also convenient. Most MIDI instruments let you program them to either accept or ignore program changes. Program changes are very good for creating subtle timbral inflections; for example, you could program four different string patches, each optimized for a specific octave range, and switch programs as the part changes from one octave to another. This approach also helps give greater expressiveness to parts played with nonvelocity sensitive keyboards.

Controller capabilities are very important. For example, if an instrument supports controller 7 as the "main volume" controller, this can be altered as needed to create pseudo-automated mixdown effects (program the volume to turn down in quiet parts and up in louder parts). However, in order to optimally use **program change** or controller changes, you really need a sequencer that lets you insert, edit, and delete these MIDI events directly . . . and most don't.

Finally, the nonstandardized instrument controllers (portamento time, filter cutoff, etc.) should be assignable to different MIDI controller numbers. (Remember, MIDI can send individual controller information for each basic channel.) Assignable controllers are great problem-solvers, since not all devices follow the de facto controller standards mentioned in Chapter 4.

Once you have a couple of MIDI keyboards, a MIDI drum machine, and some expander modules, it's time to add the heart of the MIDI studio—a MIDI sequencer.

The MIDI Sequencer

This has the same relationship to a MIDI studio as a multitrack tape recorder has to a conventional studio, and should be chosen with equal care. A MIDI sequencer lets you do lots of tricks you can't do with a normal tape recorder. There are three types of MIDI sequencers: the *add-on* sequencer for commercially available computers; the *built-in* that is part of a MIDI instrument; and the *stand-alone*, which is conceptually closest to a tape recorder. Let's look at each type.

Add-on. There is a seemingly endless stream of MIDI add-on sequencer programs: Waveform, Dr. T, MusicData, Cherry Lane, Sight & Sound, Octave-Plateau, Syntech, Yamaha, Passport, Sequential, Roland, and a zillion others seem determined to get us using personal computers as sequencers.

In many respects this is the best approach to MIDI sequencing. Although buying a computer is not a trivial investment, it represents your ticket to a number of different options. Once you have the computer, you can run several different sequencers on it to take advantage of different strengths inherent in different programs. With the IBM PC you might want to use Texture for its modular recording facilities, Sequencer Plus for its power and ease of use, or Personal Composer for its superb scoring capabilities (although of course, you cannot use more than one program at a time).

You can also run voice editors, patch librarians, and other types of music software to get more out of your original investment. And naturally, computers are suitable for all sorts of nonmusical purposes—word processing, accounting, games, telecommunications, and so on.

Finally, a computer has a monitor or TV screen—not just a little LCD display or a few LEDs—which lets you see a lot more information simultaneously and also allows for graphics.

Built-ins. Sometimes sequencers are included as part of an instrument. E-mu's Em-

ulator II, for example, includes a very complete eight-track MIDI sequencer. The Linn 9000 is another "MIDI-ready" device, which combines a high-tech drum machine with a built-in MIDI sequencer. The OB-8, when retrofitted for MIDI, can send DSX sequencer info through the OB-8 MIDI Out connector. The advantage of the built-in approach is less equipment to cart around—you don't need a separate computer, monitor, disk drive, etc.—while the disadvantage is less flexibility.

Stand-alones. Stand-alone sequencers contain a computer but are not add-ons to existing computers. They are functionally equivalent to conventional multitrack tape recorders. Although they are more convenient in some cases than add-ons (for example, switches are unambiguously labeled with their functions—with an add-on the switches are labeled with the functions of the computer), you don't have the advantage of being able to use the stand-alone for word processing and other computer functions after you're finished sequencing.

Sequencer Features

No one sequencer can be all things to all musicians. The following list, which can serve as a checklist when evaluating different models to see which one most closely meets your needs, includes some of the most common and important features you can expect to find as you look at sequencers, along with typical applications for these features. For your convenience there's a comparison sheet at the end of this section which you can photocopy and use to compare different sequencers during the buying process. Caution: As with synthesizers, not all manufacturers refer to the same feature by the same name.

Number of tracks. Sequencers typically come in 4-, 8-, 12-, 16-, and 32-track versions. I've found 8 to be adequate; but if you have several multitimbral instruments, you will find that 16 tracks is a virtual necessity. While more tracks may seem like overkill, there are some valid reasons for such things as 64-track sequencers. Even though you probably won't want to play back data to 64 different synths, these extra tracks can be

THE MIDI STUDIO / 73

used for organizing sounds. For example, with the luxury of extra tracks you could record each section of a part on its own track, which makes it easier to modify, say, just the first verse while leaving the rest of the part untouched (this can also be done with punch-in and punch-out, but separate tracks are easier to manipulate). Separate tracks can also be used for storing MIDI controller data; you might want to punch-in a difficult bend without disturbing the notes themselves, which would be recorded on a different track. The controller and note tracks could then be bounced together to create a single, composite track that contains the pitch bend *and* note data. Of course, this type of approach tends to soak up memory pretty rapidly, which is another argument in favor of getting as powerful a computer as you can afford.

Reasonably complete MIDI implementation. It's frustrating to have MIDI functions on your synthesizers that you can't access with your sequencer; the sequencer should be able to transmit and receive note on/off data plus dynamics as a bare minimum, and be capable of assigning any track to any channel. Pitch wheel change, aftertouch, and **program change**, are also very important, as is the ability to edit MIDI controller information. With respect to the latter, suppose you play a part perfectly but mess up on some of the pitch bending. If you can't edit controller information, you would need to play the entire part over again. With controller editing, you could change just the pitch bending itself.

Programmable auto-correct (also called quantization). While recording, **auto-correct** rounds off timing errors in your playing to the nearest note value you specify—quarter notes, eighth notes, triplets, etc. Generally, a high-resolution or real-time mode will also be available that turns off **auto-correct**. Some sequencers **auto-correct** only during playback, which is a useful feature since you can change **auto-correct** on an already recorded track.

Note that there are several kinds of **auto-correct**. Some quantize **note on** information but not **note off**, which can distort the note duration; others quantize both equally, which can sometimes "eat" notes; others quantize **note ons** and adjust **note offs** to maintain the same duration, which may be the most natural. (Note that the Personal Composer program provides several variables for adjusting quantization to taste.)

Disk storage option. This is a lot faster than saving data on cassettes and also more reliable—but note that speed of operation depends very much on the machine being used. C-64 disk operation is slow; Apple II disk operation is faster, but the disks don't hold that much data compared to more powerful computers. Some computers offer a hard disk option. Hard disks use a different type of technology that offers fast access and the ability to store lots of data (typically 5 to 40 Megabytes). While hard disks used to be quite costly, prices are declining rapidly.

Being able to load and save individual tracks (not just songs) to disk is also a useful feature.

Real-time, modular, and step-time programming. Real-time recording works like a tape recorder; put the sequencer into record and play away. Step-time lets you move one-step-at-a-time through each and every step of the sequence, deleting or adding notes as you see fit. Some sequencers only let you do one or the other. Modular recording lets you create individual patterns which are then linked into songs (like drum machine programming). These patterns may usually be recorded in real-time or step-time. Note that step-time, while useful, can often be simulated on real-time-only sequencers by simply slowing the tempo way down.

Punch-in and punch-out. Careful, though; there are some subtleties to MIDI punching. If you punch right after a **note on** command and don't program anything to turn that note off, the original note will sustain in the background. A preroll feature is also handy, where you can program a section to start playing a couple of measures before the punch occurs.

Automated punch-in and punch-out. This is even better. You simply program the measure and beat in the song where the punch-in and punch-out should occur, and the sequencer takes care of the rest. No more missed punches!

Programmable tempo changes. Being able to change the tempo for a song is very useful; unlike tape, speeding up and slowing down a MIDI sequencer doesn't affect the timbre of the instruments. There is one caution, though . . . if you have a densely-recorded track that is on the verge of clogging the MIDI data stream, increasing the tempo may send the program over the edge (or at least into a nervous breakdown).

Applications: Play complex parts at a slow speed, then boost the speed up for playback. Or, "humanize" a track by programming relative tempo changes (accelerando and ritardando).

Tempo tap option. Some sequencers let you set the tempo by simply tapping a button. The computer reads the time between taps, takes an average (or just gives you the time for the last two taps), and converts this time period into a beats-per-measure reading that can be used by the sequencer.

Track reassignment. Maybe you want to drive your Mirage instead of your DX-7 from track 5 without having to do any repatching . . . this option will let you do it.

Program change. This message can be recorded at any point on a MIDI channel (track) to tell a device (or devices) tuned to that channel to change programs. Optimally, you should be able to edit and manually insert program changes if desired.

Easy command language. Probably more than any other single factor, this affects how much you will enjoy using a sequencer (or any other piece of software, for that matter). You want to do the least amount of typing necessary. A program that requires only single-letter commands and lets you move a cursor around to make selections is better than one which makes you type in stuff like "SAVE: COMPOSITION #1 IN B-MINOR: DISK A." The type of "help" messages built into the program (if any) are also important. Some products aim to be so "user-friendly" that help messages are sprinkled throughout the program; this can be handy while learning but add unnecessary clutter once you know your way around a program.

Another important aspect is the clarity and appropriateness of the display screens . . . is related information grouped together? Do you have to constantly switch between screens? Is it easy to inadvertently erase tracks or, worse yet, an entire song?

Printout option. Some score/lead-sheet printout programs are better than others, but just about all of them beat doing it by hand.

Ability to name individual sequences and tracks. It's much easier to remember a song title than a number. Naming tracks is also handy; that way you know which instrument is supposed to be driven from each track.

Programmable countdown. I don't know about you, but I always need a few beats before a song starts in order to prepare myself for the recording process. Being able to start playing or recording from any bar in a song is also useful.

Programmable metronome. Being able to program fast metronome times (for example, sixteenth notes) means that you'll still have a solid click reference if you slow the sequence way down when overdubbing.

Memory expansion option. Most sequencers seem to be able to remember somewhere between 5,000 and 10,000 events (with **note on**, **note off**, pitch bend, and so on being considered as "events"). This isn't as much as it might appear to be; for example, a full second of DX-7 pitch bend can use up 2,000 events—not including the aftertouch data that was probably recorded along with the pitch bend. In fact, any dynamic controllers eat up tons of memory. Being able to expand the memory to, say, 50,000 events with an optional memory expansion package gives you a lot more space for sequences.

Memory space status. You should be able to check how much memory is left, as well as how much disk space is left.

Readable manual. Make sure the person writing the manual is trying to instruct you, not impress you. If the first few pages make good sense, the rest probably will too.

Sync-to-tape and external clock facilities. The ideal sequencer would be able to sync to anything—MIDI timing information, SMPTE, click pulses, and so on. Generally, sequencers don't have all these capabilities, although you can usually find a suitable adapter box (from the likes of J. L. Cooper, Roland, Garfield Electronics, Synchronous Technologies, etc.) for specific situations.

Nondestructive editing. When editing a sequence, some sequencers create a copy for you to edit. This preserves an unedited version of the original in case you end up not liking the edited sequence as much (don't you wish tape recorders would save a previous track when you did an overdub?). When you get an edited version you prefer, you can then overwrite the original. Even if a sequencer does not offer this feature, you can usually approximate this function by saving a track to the disk (program permitting), so that you always have a back-up of the original, or by copying to another track and muting the original track as you work on the revised version.

Fast forward/rewind. It's fun to hear the sequence whiz by as you look for a part towards the beginning or end of a song.

Search. Search looks for a particular part of the sequence or places you a certain number of measures into the sequence.

Bounce. You should be able to bounce data for tracks around and to combine tracks together. However, remember that tracks that are bounced together cannot be unbounced.

Applications: Play individual sections of a complex part for one instrument over several tracks, then bounce them all down to create one composite part on one track. Also, play several different solos on multiple tracks, then use punch-in and punch-out to erase those parts of the solo you don't like and bounce the sections that remain into one track, thus freeing up the other tracks for more instruments.

Offset. Some sequencers let you offset one track from another in single clock pulse increments (i.e., $1/24$th of a beat since MIDI is a 24 pulses-per-quarter-note system). If you don't have direct offset, you can often fake it by inserting a short bar (one thirty-second note, for example) in front of a copy of a nonoffset track. Rather than an overall track offset, some programs have *time-offset* filters, which let you change only selected parts of a track.

Applications: "Tune out" timing differences between devices whose computers exhibit timing lags to obtain perfect synchronization. Or, create special effects such as doubling, chorusing, echo, canon harmonies, and arpeggiation by copying a track to another track and offsetting the new track by the desired amount compared to the old track.

Transpose. So you can't sing that song in D sharp after all? Then transpose until you hit the right range. Some programs offer both individual track transpose and overall song transpose.

Filter. The filtering function eliminates selected data from the MIDI data stream.

Applications: Suppose you played left- and right-hand parts on a single keyboard and wanted to split off the left-hand part to a different keyboard. You could copy the track and filter the low notes from the original, thus sending the right-hand part to one instrument. The next step would be to filter the high notes from the copy and send the low notes (the left-hand part) to a different instrument. (I first saw this particular low-note/high-note filtering option in Roger Powell's Texture program.)

Another use for filtering is to conserve memory. Aftertouch, pitch bend, velocity, and similar real-time data take up a fair amount of sequencer memory. Filtering out data that is not used in a performance makes more memory available for other functions and sequences.

Filters aren't just for conserving memory, however. If you record several tracks full of aftertouch and other dynamic controllers, you can quickly end up with a song that is not playable through a single MIDI Out. Imagine what happens when four complex tracks are recorded singly, then played back together . . . MIDI data stream clogging is a real problem, and filters are about the only good cure.

There are two kinds of filters: one filter blocks on **record** (for example, it ignores all controllers); another removes data from already-recorded tracks. This is similar to record versus playback auto-correct—**record** filtering is useful when you know you don't want aftertouch, and track filters can take a lot of time to remove data (if you're going to filter out 300 bars chock-full of aftertouch data, it might be time for a break).

Mute/cue function. This lets you selectively silence tracks while recording or playing back. Some programs let you mute/un-mute during playback, while others let you make these changes only while the sequence is stopped. (Note: The more features that are available while the record or playback process is in progress, the better.)

Application: Record four or five different solos, and listen to each one individually before deciding which one to keep. For live use this means you can play different solos at different performances so you don't get bored with hearing the same sequenced part over and over and over and over again.

Low-cost software updates. According to Anderton's Law of High-Tech Equipment Purchasing, never buy anything that says Version 1.0 unless the company will upgrade you to the next software revision for a reasonably low fee. Initial software offerings often have bugs; by the time you get to version 1.4 or so, the bugs are pretty much all gone. Note that software upgrades are much more common, less expensive, and easier to install if you have an add-on sequencer as opposed to a built-in or stand-alone type.

Copy protection. Copy protection means that the disk cannot be duplicated or copied over to another disk. This prevents people from ripping off the program and making unauthorized copies, but it also prevents legitimate users from making back-up copies to guard against damage to a master disk. Also, you usually can't use a hard disk with copy-protected software because the software can't be copied over to the hard disk. Although copy protection is a pain, I would be the last person to advocate the elimination of copy-protected disks—writing software takes a tremendous amount of time and money, and people who rip off a program are no better than shoplifters or car thieves.

Check the manufacturer's policies toward providing back-up copies in case your master gets trashed; you shouldn't have to pay list price twice for the same program, although the level of manufacturer paranoia varies widely.

Sequencer Comparison Checklist

Use the checklist on the following page, in conjunction with the above explanations of features, to help you decide which sequencer is correct for your particular application.

Synchronizing to Tape

Synchronizing a MIDI sequencer to tape gives even more flexibility: you can record electronic MIDI instruments on the MIDI sequencer and acoustic instruments on the multitrack recorder, then during mixdown run the two simultaneously to obtain more tracks than you could obtain with either recorder by itself. The tracks recorded in the sequencer are often called *virtual tracks*, since they fulfill the exact same function as tracks recorded on tape yet are not recorded on tape.

Many sequencers have sync-to-tape facilities built in, which certainly makes life convenient. In fact, for most synchronization applications the sequencer's sync-to-tape is all you'll ever need. These days, though, life does not involve only audio; there's also video. So we might want to sync a sequencer, audio recorder, and video recorder together . . . which brings us to SMPTE time code.

Although there are several timing standards (Chapter 1 covered the use of click tracks and FSK synchronization; and of course, in Chapter 4 we talked about MIDI synchronization signals), for most professional videotape editing and multitrack synchronization applications, SMPTE time code is the sync standard of choice. Originally developed by NASA as a means of accurately logging data, SMPTE time code labels each frame of a videotape by recording a unique piece of digital data on that frame. For American (NTSC standard) television and video, each second of SMPTE time code is divided into 30 frames (the standard number of frames that pass by in 1 second of video; the standard frame rate for film is 24 frames per second, and for European television and video, 25 frames per second). Each frame is further divided into 80 subframes, with each subframe being 0.417 milliseconds long. A typical time code location might be 00:10:08:29:(76), which you would read as 00 hours, 10 minutes, 8 seconds, 29 frames, and 76 subframes into the videotape. There are other variations on SMPTE time code, such as the notorious "drop frame" mode, but we have enough to think about for now.

The SMPTE time code emanating from a SMPTE generator can be recorded on tape and played back into a SMPTE time code reader, which precisely identifies where you are on the tape. This data not only helps synchronize audio to video but can also synchronize two or more audio recorders together. Instruments that read SMPTE, such

Sequencer Comparison Checklist

	Sequencer A	Sequencer B	Sequencer C
Number of tracks	_____	_____	_____
(Answer the following with Y or N.)			
Auto-correct	_____	_____	_____
Disk storage	_____	_____	_____
Real-time progamming	_____	_____	_____
Modular programming	_____	_____	_____
Step-time programming	_____	_____	_____
Punch-in/punch-out	_____	_____	_____
Automated punching	_____	_____	_____
Programmed tempo changes	_____	_____	_____
Tempo tap option	_____	_____	_____
Track reassignment	_____	_____	_____
Printout option	_____	_____	_____
Name sequences/tracks	_____	_____	_____
Programmable countdown	_____	_____	_____
Programmable metronome	_____	_____	_____
Memory expansion option	_____	_____	_____
Memory space status	_____	_____	_____
Sync-to-tape	_____	_____	_____
Accepts external clock pulses	_____	_____	_____
Accepts SMPTE clock	_____	_____	_____
Accepts MIDI clock	_____	_____	_____
Nondestructive editing	_____	_____	_____
Fast forward/rewind	_____	_____	_____
Search	_____	_____	_____
Bounce	_____	_____	_____
Offset	_____	_____	_____
Transpose	_____	_____	_____
Filter aftertouch	_____	_____	_____
Filter velocity	_____	_____	_____
Filter pitch bend	_____	_____	_____
Filter real-time data	_____	_____	_____
Filter modulation	_____	_____	_____
Filter note ranges	_____	_____	_____
Mute/cue	_____	_____	_____
Free software updates	_____	_____	_____
Copy protection	_____	_____	_____
(Rate the following from 1 to 5 with 1 = excellent and 5 = poor.)			
Readable manual	_____	_____	_____
MIDI implementation	_____	_____	_____
Easy commands	_____	_____	_____

as the Emulator II, can be easily synchronized to the SMPTE time code signal.

So how does this relate to MIDI? There are now several SMPTE to MIDI synchronizers that can translate the SMPTE time code reading into how many MIDI beats (timing pulses) have elapsed since the beginning of the tape. A MIDI sequencer can use this information to align itself with the tape so that, if you start the tape at, say, beat 2 of measure 45 of a composition, the sequencer will also start playing from beat 2 of measure 45. Therefore, you can start the tape rolling at any point; and within a fraction of a second, any sequencer or drum machine that responds to **song position pointer** information will "know" where it should be in the sequence relative to the time code and will start playing from that point.

If the beginning of the tape is not at the same point as the beginning of the composition, no problem. Most synchronizers have *offset registers* that will cause the external sync pulses to start when the SMPTE reader reaches a specified number.

Incidentally, sound designer Frank Serafine has a low-tech way to synchronize SMPTE and MIDI without the use of an external box. He simply records two sync tracks—one that drives MIDI devices and one that drives SMPTE devices—on adjacent tracks of a multitrack recorder. Thus, the two timing tracks are always in sync with each other; and he can always relate the MIDI timing information to SMPTE timing information recorded on the next track over.

Although many people think SMPTE is the wave of the future, at present it is relatively expensive to implement and does have some limitations (see sidebar).

Hooking It All Up

Now that we have our tools together, let's hook everything up. **Fig. 7-1** shows a typical four-track MIDI studio setup. The MIDI signal from the computer interface or sequencer goes to Synth 1's MIDI In. A replica of the signal entering Synth 1's MIDI In is available at the MIDI Thru connector (sort of like the "dry out" or "direct out" found in effects boxes), which we use to also send the computer data to Synth 2. By feeding MIDI Thru

---

SMPTE in the Real World

Going SMPTE costs money—starting at about $1000 and increasing from there. However, SMPTE is also an investment in the future. Its ability to synchronize multiple tape decks or video/audio equipment is invaluable when doing jingle work, industrial presentations, videos, and so on. One SMPTE device, the SMPL System from Synchronous Technologies, goes so far as to provide automated tape control, automatic punch-in/punch-out and muting, and several other features.

One reason why SMPTE is expensive is because of features needed for professional production work. For example, having to maintain a strict tempo throughout a commercial can be a real problem, since you might want to "fudge" the tempo a bit so that audio cues match up precisely with video cues. Some currently available SMPTE sync units, such as the Roland SBX-80 and Garfield Master Beat, include a *beat map* capability where you can tap exactly where beats should fall (or numerically enter where the beats should fall).

When it comes to SPTE/MIDI sync, there are some problems that must be considered. For SMPTE to relate to MIDI, MIDI song position information must be correlated to SMPTE frame information. If the MIDI device doesn't include song position—and many don't—auto-locating MIDI devices to SMPTE becomes impractical. Another problem is the 24 ppqn MIDI clock, which doesn't offer enough resolution to provide an event at every possible place you might want an event. Finally, SMPTE/MIDI sync boxes usually can't talk to the computer running the MIDI sequencer, which makes using these boxes more tedious than they should be (i.e., you have to keep entering offset points and cuing up the sequence by hand).

Nonetheless, SMPTE/MIDI converters are a virtual necessity if you plan to get into serious video/audio production. The main point is that, because going SMPTE is costly, buying decisions become more critical than ever before . . . as one example, you had better make sure that your MIDI sequencer can indeed respond to **song pointer** information.

---

jacks to MIDI In jacks, we can send the computer data to several slaves. Note that, if you are willing to settle for single-note melody lines, instead of using four separate synths you could use one four-voice multitimbral synthesizer.

However, as we all know, MIDI is not perfect; some instruments do not provide MIDI Thru jacks, and daisy-chaining too

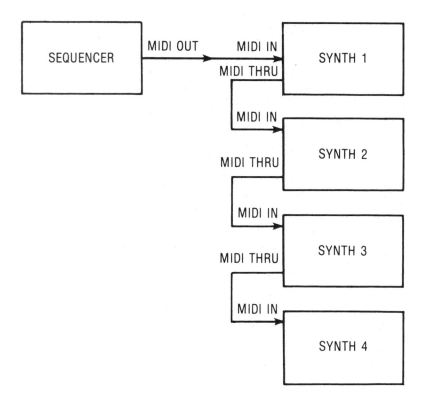

Figure 7–1

many devices can lead to data distortion. In fact, the setup shown in **Fig. 7-1** could very easily not work reliably if the cables are too long or made of the wrong materials, or if certain instruments have marginal components. Fortunately, a MIDI Thru accessory box (as mentioned in Chapter 6; see **Fig. 6-2**) can provide an individual MIDI Out signal to each instrument. Each MIDI Out connects to an instrument's MIDI In jack. Several companies make MIDI Thru boxes with four to eight outputs for those who really want to stretch their studio; these are often cascadable if you need to drive more than eight instruments.

You should also consider your studio's layout. The keyboard needs to be very accessible, so you might want to invest in a master remote keyboard and MIDI signal switcher to prevent having to jump around from keyboard to keyboard when programming different parts. The main computer box usually doesn't have to be accessed very much, but the disk drives should be reasonably easy to get to—on a shelf underneath your playing surface, for example. Just remember to keep sensitive gear off the floor, as dust can cause real problems.

The monitor should be easily visible from anywhere in the studio (which makes swivel stands a good idea). However, televisions and computers can generate a fair amount of interference, so you probably won't want them too close to high-gain transducers such as tape heads and guitar pickups. If you have good hearing, the TV's high-frequency horizontal oscillator can drive you nuts—one of those little LCD TVs might be a better alternative. Although it is not as visible as a standard monitor, at least it is real portable so you can take it to wherever you are (cables permitting).

Learning the MIDI Studio

Congratulations! Everything is in place and ready to go. Dig out the sequencer's owner manual and start putting the machine through its paces. Remember to set your MIDI channels and modes (Omni On or Off; Poly or Mono) correctly, and you'll be off to a good start.

Not everything will go smoothly, of course. You should be prepared for surprises (both good and bad) and some frustration. Remember those times your tape recorder wouldn't record—until you noticed that you were in sync mode? Those kinds of beginner's mistakes are very common when using MIDI. MIDI has so many variables that things seldom work perfectly from the beginning. You will have to make sure that your controllers are set so that they can talk to the sequencer, and you might occasionally run into a hardware or software bug. These are part of the deal, just like a drop-out on regular tape. The important thing is not to give up or to let frustration take the upper hand. Come back later with a fresh outlook, study the manual a little further, and experiment.

Once you begin to use the MIDI studio, you'll really start to appreciate how much it simplifies and speeds up the composition process. Given the current state of technology, this is about as close as you're going to come to the tapeless studio. If you've been looking for something truly new in musical electronics, look no further; the MIDI studio will be a fertile ground for experimentation in the years ahead.

Chapter 8

MIDI Accessories

There are many accessories that can enhance the performance of a MIDI system; of these, the absolutely most powerful accessory is a personal computer with MIDI compatibility. We will begin this chapter with a look at several popular computers, then move along to other accessories.

MIDI Computers

Computers are great. Even without the added incentive of using a computer for MIDI applications, they are incredibly powerful tools. I write all my books and articles on a computer, send electronic mail to other musicians via modem, and keep all my business records on a spreadsheet. (And when I'm designing a circuit, that same spreadsheet program also calculates the proper capacitor values needed to obtain a particular frequency response.)

But even if you have no interest in computers other than for musical applications, they're worth the investment. There are many ways to interface a computer to MIDI devices (remember all those software-based applications in Chapter 6, such as patch library programs?) to improve performance or make life easier for you.

Some computers (such as the Atari ST series and Yamaha CX5M) already include a built-in MIDI port, but these relatively new computers were designed since the advent of MIDI. Older computers do not have MIDI ports; but luckily, several add-on products can translate computer data into a MIDI-compatible format (and of course, translate MIDI data into signals the computer can understand). These *MIDI computer interfaces* are available from a number of companies (Hybrid Arts, MusicData, Passport Designs, Sequential, Syntech, Assimilation Systems, etc. etc. etc.) for anywhere from about $70 to $200. The interface plugs into one of the computer's existing connectors and provides MIDI Out and MIDI In connectors for accessing the computer (note that a few interfaces only provide MIDI Out; these are nowhere near as useful, so avoid them). Whether you have an Apple, Commodore, IBM, or other computer, chances are there's an interface available that will give the computer MIDI capabilities.

The above interfaces are all considered "dumb" interfaces because they simply handle data communications without adding any intelligent processing of their own. However, Roland's MPU-401 "smart" interface includes its own processor, which handles a lot of chores for the programmer. This interface is required in order to run some of the more powerful sequencer programs, such as MPS, Personal Composer, Sequencer Plus, and Texture. Those who are interested in more specifics should look at the sidebar.

Choosing a computer for musical applications is not an easy task, which is compounded by the rapid rate of change in the industry. Although much of the following information could be out of date shortly, we may get lucky; several industry insiders have told me to expect a period of relative stability. This is partly because developing software takes a huge amount of time and effort, so software companies would like to see some stability in the market so that products can have longer useful lives. Computer manufacturers are also more conscientious about making machines that can accept older as well as newer software; for example, the Commodore 128 accepts Commodore 64 software so that Commodore 64 owners who want to trade up to the more powerful model will not have obsolete software on their hands. Likewise, IBM's AT can run IBM PC software.

The Roland MPU-401

The MPU-401 can do the following:

- Handle record, playback, and punching for eight (or more if you know how) separate tracks simultaneously.
- Buffer data individually for each track, while either transmitting or receiving, so that the host computer need not drop everything the instant a new MIDI message comes in. This allows for playback from disk, with truly huge numbers of notes (although no commercial product does this yet).
- Handle tempo changes, accelerandos, and ritardandos automatically.
- Filter out MIDI controllers, **system exclusive** commands, and **active sensing**.
- Generate a metronome automatically.
- Provide an overall musically-relevant timebase (the MPU interrupts the host computer each sixteenth note—or whatever is desired—to update the clock, change screen graphics, or perform similar housekeeping functions).
- Provide FSK sync-to-tape. The internal time-base is programmable from 24 to 192 ppqn, with 7 increments. An internal phase-locked-loop lets it sync to external MIDI clocks at 24 ppqn and still use 96 ppqn (or whatever is desired) internally. This gives the advantage of a high-resolution clock within a MIDI system.
- Refer to *channel reference tables* when combining two or more MIDI tracks onto the same channel or merging MIDI In data (from keyboard) with sequencer data for playback on the same synth. This creates "MIDI multiple triggers" so that overlapping notes (same pitch, but from different sources) don't truncate each other or cause weird effects.
- Perform the above tasks without involving the host computer in these kind of details, so that the computer can do more high-level editing, playback, user support, or whatever.

In theory, up to four MPU-401s can be connected together in order to support up to four separate MIDI connections; this has not yet been done commercially, however, since modifications to the board within the MPU-401 are required and, also, since writing software for this kind of task is pretty complicated.

The MPU-401 has established an industry standard that will probably be around for at least a few more years. Earlier bugs have been fixed on the current version (Revision 1.5). Also, the documentation—not exactly a model of clarity—is being revised, and the new version should be available when this book hits the streets.

One important point is to plan ahead for future expansion. People traditionally underestimate the computing power they need; although you can get a lot out of consumer-oriented "toy" computers, a more powerful computer gives more powerful results. Even if you do expand, though, chances are you'll want to hold on to your older computer. Suppose you bought a C-64 and now want a better machine for more powerful sequencing: simply dedicate the C-64 to handling patch library software and the like; or for that matter, use it as a controller for a home security system.

The computers mentioned below are either well-established and well-supported, or acknowledged as up-and-coming machines with a good chance for widespread acceptance. Although you will need additional information before you can make a truly informed buying decision (specifications are subject to change without notice, and new models continue to appear), hopefully the following profiles will help point you in the right direction.

One general comment about computers is that the more memory, the better. A sequencer designed to run with a computer having 64K of memory will typically store 3000 to 5000 notes—enough for a few songs but not enough for an entire set. A 512K computer, on the other hand, stores tens of thousands of notes. Of course, you pay more for the privilege of extra storage; however some computers can be easily expanded from their initial memory configuration (the Apple II, for instance, can expand from 64K to 128K and the Amiga from 256K to 8 *Mega*bytes). Extra memory also allows more program features and a much friendlier user interface; with a 64K or 128K computer, the program size is quite limited, thus leaving little room for graphics, on-line help, error-checking, and so on.

Apple II/IIc/IIe Family

Many musicians already have an Apple II or IIe, which is supported by thousands of available programs and add-on accessories (including over two dozen MIDI software packages). It is usable for business applications, makes an excellent home computer, and is not too expensive if you can find one on sale or secondhand. A big attraction is that the data buss accepts a number of optional plug-in circuit boards ("cards"), and you can change the "personality" of the computer simply by plugging in different cards. This is referred to as an *open* system. For example, if you plug in a card with drum synthesizer circuitry on it, the computer can control drum sounds. In addition to the cards manufactured by Apple, there are literally hundreds of other cards available from other manufacturers.

Even the oldest Apple II can be upgraded; but if you're buying a computer for the first time, you will probably want to start off with the Apple IIe, an enhanced version of the original Apple. The Apple IIc is a small, elegant, portable computer that is eminently suitable for road use. However, it does not run all programs available for the Apple II and IIe family, is not an open system, and just recently became MIDI-capable.

But the Apple II's big advantage—being an established, well-supported machine—has a flip side. The basic technology is almost a decade old; and although the Apple IIe has extended the overall performance, its 8-bit/limited memory architecture can't handle the kind of programs that run on the 32-bit Mac or Amiga. The Apple II disk drives are slow (although not as slow as the Commodore 64 drives) and hold only about 170K of data (newer drives used with other machines can hold up to 1 Megabyte).

Apple Macintosh

Apple's Macintosh is rapidly becoming the "artist's favorite" because of its sleek packaging and the MacPaint program; MIDI software, initially slow in coming, now numbers about a half-dozen programs. The Mac is not perfect, however. It is relatively expensive; the disk drive can be slow (although not as slow as the Commodore 64's disk drive); and it's not an open system. Considering how much the open nature of the Apple II contributed to its success, it's difficult to understand why Apple didn't take this approach with the Mac. There are several "fixes" for

the Mac to help overcome some of its limitations, including a hard disk drive that mounts inside the case and memory-expansion boards. These enhancements are fairly expensive.

The Mac has some stunning advantages, though. Its graphic abilities, coupled with Apple's high-resolution laser printer, seem ideally suited for lead sheeting and transcription (assuming that suitable software exists for your application). The Mac is also easy to use; it offers reasonable capabilities as a small business computer; and its compact construction makes it an unobtrusive addition to your studio or workplace. Only time will tell whether the Mac gets the software and market support it needs to become a true workhorse in the fickle personal computer market and whether it can hold its own against newer, sexier computers.

Atari ST

The Atari ST has been introduced so recently I haven't had a chance to check it out. But the preliminary buzz is interesting: it is very inexpensive and includes a built-in MIDI interface. This is a "dumb" interface with some simple internal software support (such as send and receive data); there is no provision for synchronizing to external signals. There doesn't appear to be a way to add more MIDI ports or hook in an intelligent interface like the MPU-401; and the unit itself doesn't seem to be overly expandable— the expansion port is for a 192K ROM cartridge, with no apparent provision for an external "open slot" expander box like the Amiga. Still, considering that you get a computer with many of the Macintosh's capabilities for under $800, this is a machine that could make some big waves in the consumer market (not unlike the Commodore 64 did when it was first introduced).

Commodore 64, 128, and Amiga

Commodore's C-64 is a wonderful game machine; it is inexpensive; and there's lots of available software. Although it is less "pro" than Apple or IBM computers, its power should not be underestimated. For those on a budget, the Commodore 64 is an ideal way to get involved in MIDI work; and like the Apple, there are over two dozen software packages written with the C-64 in mind. Some of these programs are real works of art, in that they squeeze every single last byte of performance out of an already fairly capable—but inherently limited—machine. Of course, you can't expect anywhere near the same quality of performance as an Amiga, Mac, or IBM PC; but the C-64 offers an economical entry into computing for those on a very tight budget.

Another point to consider is that used C-64s are often available at a very reasonable price. This is because many people got sucked into the "every home should have a home computer" hype of the late 70s, only to find out that making it do really useful tasks takes some time and effort. Keep your eyes on the classified ads in your local paper; I've seen complete Commodore systems (computer, disk drive, monitor, printer, and some software) going for as little as $300 to $400. The SX-64, a portable version of the C-64, includes a built-in monitor and disk drive and often sells for under $400.

Incidentally, the C-64 was the first machine to include a decent-sounding on-board sound synthesizer. Although later eclipsed by the sound generators in such machines as the CX5M and Amiga, the C-64 can still create some pretty good sounds. As a result, there are many inexpensive programs that have nothing to do with MIDI and simply let you access the internal sound-generating chip. One of the best features of the sound chip is that it offers a great deal of resolution—notes can be as little as 0.061 Hz apart—making the C-64 ideal for experimentation with alternate tuning systems (such as just intonation and microtonal tunings).

The C-128 is a more businesslike computer that has 128K of memory; it will run older C-64 software in addition to C-128 and CP/M software (the latter is designed primarily for business applications). If your interest is music software, the modestly-priced C-128 is as good a bet as the C-64 and is a much better bet if you plan to use the C-128's additional capabilities. Remember, though, that C-64 software is written with a

64K machine in mind and therefore does not use the additional 64K of memory to good advantage.

Commodore's Amiga looks *extremely* promising for musical applications. It has twin on-board four-voice synthesizers (which are also used for speech synthesis) and can even sample sounds into memory. The graphics capabilities are superb; the cost is reasonable; expansion is possible at slight extra cost; and the machine itself is technically advanced. However, there is some question as to how long it will take for the Amiga to be as well-supported as the Apple II and C-64. As of this writing, the Amiga was just shown publicly for the first time last month, so details are sketchy. Commodore does have a lot riding on this machine, though, so I presume they will be trying to get software support up to speed as soon as humanly possible. Many engineers, artists, software developers, and musicians (myself included) are hoping that the Amiga will be a success— but that question will be decided by a marketplace which some consider to be already close to saturated.

IBM PC

The IBM PC has about a half-dozen MIDI software programs available, as well as tons of business software and even an excellent flight-simulator program. Although it was not particularly cost-effective upon its introduction, recent price cuts (spurred by competition) have brought prices down to a very reasonable level. Hard disks are quite inexpensive as well, especially compared to offerings for the Apple II and Macintosh.

If you are interested in a PC, also consider the PC's "clones" (computers, produced by other manufacturers, which are generally conceded as more cost-effective than IBM's offerings). Unfortunately, some of these clones are not 100 percent compatible with the IBM PC; the only way to be sure the clone will work for your application is to run the software you're planning to use on the compatible machine. If everything works— and it will most of the time—great. If not, you'll need to pay the price for IBM's model.

PCs have some other advantages. The standardized architecture is well documented, and competition has helped to give more value for money. Graphics capabilities are quite good, and there is no doubt that the PC is a more powerful machine than the Apple II family or Commodore. However, the music community has been slow to embrace the PC. Early music programs, which were relatively simple, didn't need a particularly powerful computer; and now that the market has become more sophisticated, the trend seems to be turning towards newer 32-bit machines like the Mac and Amiga.

Yamaha CX5M

Yamaha's MSX-compatible CX5M is a "musician's computer" designed specifically to augment Yamaha equipment. It's not a bad machine at all; but it is the least supported of all the computers mentioned because the MSX software standard has not had much impact in the U.S. In fact, most people I know haven't even heard of it, so a few words of background might be in order. MSX is an operating system designed by Microsoft, an American software company, in conjunction with several Japanese computer makers. Computers that follow the MSX standard can readily talk to each other, and peripherals that work with one manufacturer's MSX computer will work with any other MSX computer. At this point the MSX standard is fairly old, so it is unlikely that there will be significant support for MSX machines in the U.S. A revised standard, MSX II, is on the way; but it could be too little and too late to do much good.

The CX5M's biggest selling points are the built-in MIDI interface and sound generator. The sound generator gives essentially the same capabilities as a Yamaha DX9 keyboard; add on one of two optional keyboards (minikeys or regular-size keys), and you've got an eight-voice polyphonic synthesizer with 48 different preprogrammed sounds. While certain basic features are lacking (the keyboards provide neither dynamics nor pitch-bend controllers; all programs must at present be saved to cassette; and there is a miniscule 32K of RAM), the CX5M is adequate for working out songs and doing basic composition.

The only software available right now comes from Yamaha; the selection includes a sequencer, programming utility for the DX-7, and a programming utility that maximizes the usefulness of the CX5M's internal voice chip. Whether much outside software will become available for the CX5M is not clear at this point, but anything is possible.

So which computer is right for you? Beats me! With so many choices, you must carefully analyze your needs and check over the available features. My own computer roster includes a Viasyn/CompuPro machine for business work that has nothing to do with MIDI software; it's an industrial-strength computer that is faster than lightning and incredibly reliable. I also have a Commodore 64 for music and recording work, which has served me very well and has had none of the reliability problems that some owners have reported. (If you're seriously into computers, I think it makes sense to choose separate models for business and music, since it's hard for one computer to be all things to all applications.) While on the road, I work with a laptop computer and load the data into my CompuPro when I get home. My most recent acquisition was a Macintosh, because I needed something with real good graphics that could run sophisticated music software. When the Amiga comes out, you can bet I'll be taking a close look at that as well, especially if it becomes the "in" computer for music applications. Decisions, decisions . . . all I can say is that, if you don't have a computer, almost any computer is better than no computer at all.

MIDI Switch

After all that high-tech computer talk, let's consider the simplest, least expensive MIDI device going: an on/off switch inserted in the MIDI line. Sure, it sounds trivial; but this accessory has several applications. Suppose you're slaving two keyboards together and, for some songs, want the slave keyboard off. Although you could accomplish this by pulling out the MIDI cord, turning down the slave volume, or assigning the two synths to Poly mode and changing the channel assignment on the master, it's much simpler to just flick a switch that interrupts the flow of MIDI information from one device to another. One caution: Don't turn the switch off while the slave is playing any notes, or those notes will be stuck on since they will have no way to receive **note off** messages.

MIDI Filters

You might not always want a device to receive all available MIDI data; the MIDI filter removes certain types of information from the MIDI data stream while leaving everything else intact.

As one application, suppose you want to overdub a sequencer track using a mother keyboard that transmits aftertouch information. Unfortunately, transmitting these parameters along with the note on/off and pitch bend information uses up too much sequencer memory. Inserting a MIDI Filter between the keyboard's MIDI Out and sequencer's MIDI In solves the problem by removing the aftertouch information. As mentioned previously, many sequencers already include the ability to selectively filter certain types of MIDI data.

Perhaps an even more important application is to reduce the MIDI data stream clogging we've referred to at several different points in this book. Filtering out unnecessary data from the data stream makes the whole system work more reliably and efficiently.

MIDI Patch Bays

No, these are not patch bays controlled via MIDI (maybe next year). Instead, the MIDI patch bay serves as a "traffic manager" for the data flowing to and from multiple MIDI instruments. A typical MIDI patch bay accommodates four to eight MIDI devices, and provides some means of programming the MIDI signal paths (usually via switches) so that any device can serve as either a master or slave.

To illustrate the use of this accessory, suppose you have a DX-7, Casio CZ-101, MIDI drum machine, and sequencer. To record a DX-7 part into sequencer track 1, switch the DX-7 to **master** and play away. To record track 2, since the DX-7 cannot at present transmit on channel 2, either keep the DX-7 as the master and add a "channelizing" accessory (described later), or switch the CZ-101 (with its funky keyboard) into the **master**

position. Now let's suppose you want to program the drums using the DX-7's velocity capabilities. Select the DX-7 as the master and the drums as the slave. Finally, after recording all the parts you want into the sequencer, select the sequencer as the master and use the other instruments as sequencer-controlled slaves.

MIDI patch bays can be simple, inexpensive designs; or they can be computerized gizmos capable of remembering particular master/slave combinations that can be recalled at the touch of a button. I've even seen some MIDI patch bays with wireless remote control so that you don't even have to walk over to the patch bay and flick a switch. Of course, this kind of decadence costs—and a simple unit will handle most of your needs.

The MIDI Thru Box

This is about as close as you can come to the universal do-all, fix-all box. As we mentioned in Chapters 6 and 7, daisy-chaining a bunch of devices via their MIDI Thru jacks can cause problems such as data distortion where the MIDI data is somewhat degraded every time it passes through an instrument's MIDI interface. By the time the signal has gone through four or five units, the amount of degradation might be sufficient to cause some real problems, such as occasional dropped notes.

The MIDI Thru box takes care of these problems by splitting a MIDI input into several independent, buffered MIDI Out signals. Because these are "first-generation" MIDI signals, they are much cleaner than signals that have worked their way through several MIDI interfaces. Interestingly, musicians who originally added MIDI Thru boxes to their systems solely in order to drive more MIDI instruments from a single output have reported other improvements, such as faster response times.

MIDI Thru boxes are available in everything from 4 channel to 16 channel versions.

Exotic MIDI Connectors

MIDI cables should be less than 15 meters (50 feet) long, because cables have inherent capacitance which can interfere with proper data transfer. The longer the cable, the greater the capacitance; and therefore the greater the potential for problems.

One solution is the fiber optic MIDI cable. Fiber optic cables (originally developed for carrying digital telephone communications without loss) transmit light, which is not affected by cable capacitance. However, this approach is not cheap; fiber optics requires a transducer to convert MIDI signals to pulsed light, and another transducer to convert the pulsed light back into MIDI signals.

Wireless MIDI setups offer the ultimate in flexibility. These resemble the wireless units commonly used by guitarists and singers, except that MIDI wireless units transmit digital data instead of audio. Wireless technology is even more expensive than fiber optics, though; count on spending a good $1,000 to $2,000.

Power Line Conditioners

Since so much MIDI equipment is computer-based, and since computers can be sensitive to line voltage variations, consider adding a device to your system that isolates electrical equipment from the ill effects of AC voltage variations. *Line filters* and *surge suppressors* "soak up" transient, high-level signals that occasionally appear on the AC line (usually when a current-hungry device on the same line turns on or off). If you're interested in building your own, check out Steve Ciarcia's article on the subject in the December 1983 issue of *Byte* magazine.

If your instruments lose their memory (or their minds, for that matter) when accidentally turned off, and if you're independently wealthy, check out the *uninterruptible power supply*. These keep equipment alive for a certain period of time after power has been removed; they were originally designed with computer owners in mind, since computers often keep data in *volatile* memory (i.e., memory in which data is lost when the power is removed).

Sync Boxes

These were covered in more detail in the previous chapter on MIDI recording, where we looked at the sync box's ability to change SMPTE data to MIDI **song position pointer**

data. The important point to remember is that MIDI is only one form of synchronization, and you might need to synchronize MIDI devices to other timing standards (such as the SMPTE code used in film and video work). Several manufacturers make sync boxes that convert SMPTE time code references to MIDI timing information.

The Family of J. L. Cooper "Problem-Solver" Boxes

J. L. Cooper Electronics is probably the most prolific company in the MIDI accessory biz. Their product development process is simple: musicians describe their problems, and Jim Cooper comes up with an appropriate solution. The remaining hardware products in this section are all made by J. L. Cooper, but please note that some functions are duplicated by other manufacturers' products.

MIDI Data Mixer

The MIDI data mixer combines the MIDI Out data from two different devices and creates a single MIDI Out containing the composite data. The Cooper MIDI Data Mixer also allows certain types of data (aftertouch, velocity, etc.) to be filtered out of the data stream.

Should you want to control a single multitimbral expander from two keyboards played by two keyboardists, a MIDI data mixer can combine the MIDI Out data from two mother keyboards and present this data stream to the expander's MIDI In connector.

MIDI CV Out

Remember way back in the first chapter where we talked about synthesizers that interface via control voltage and gate signals instead of MIDI? The MIDI CV Out can "listen" to any of the 16 MIDI basic channels and provide appropriate gate and control voltage outputs for driving older synthesizers (such as the minimoog). For example, if the MIDI signal says to play A 440, the MIDI CV Out sends out a control voltage that will cause the older synthesizer to play A 440. One of the cute features of this box is that if it receives more than one note at once, you can program it to send out either the lowest note, the highest note, or the last note played.

MIDI CV In

This is similar to the MIDI CV Out but works in reverse—specifically, it slaves a MIDI device to a master device that sends out control voltage and gate outputs. You simply feed the control voltage and gate signals into the box, then select the channel over which you want the MIDI data to appear.

MIDI Sync-I

Suppose you have an older drum unit or sequencer that doesn't provide MIDI but does send out a 24, 48, or 96 pulses-per-quarter-note clock pulse. The MIDI Sync-I converts this pulse stream into MIDI clock information suitable for driving MIDI gear that responds to timing data.

MIDINTERFACE I-Out

Feeding a MIDI signal into this adapter produces up to eight independent channels of control voltages and gates. Thus, older polyphonic synthesizers with CV and gate inputs can be slaved to MIDI systems. MIDI pitch bend and modulation information is also converted to control voltage variations.

MIDINTERFACE I-In

This is a reverse MIDINTERFACE I-Out that converts up to eight CV and gate signals into a single MIDI output. Thus, newer MIDI gear can be slaved to older sequencers with CV/gate outputs, such as the Oberheim DSX and Roland MC-4. A similar but less general-purpose product, the Oberface, interfaces the Oberheim DSX sequencer to MIDI equipment. All the DSX functions work exactly as normal. MIDI capabilities include the ability to store two groups of notes ("main" notes and "auxiliary" notes) on different MIDI channels; furthermore, these groups can be split into two channels with four voices each. Since the DSX cannot store velocity or pitch bend information, these functions are not available for MIDI equipment connected to the DSX.

Braindriver

Many Simmons-type drum machines have sequencer-based "brains" that are programmed by playing drum pads. The Braindriver accepts MIDI signals and provides 12 channels of independent pulses, which can be fed into the drum unit's brain. Thus, electric drums can be easily programmed from keyboards or sequencers.

Drumslave

This essentially does the opposite of the Braindriver; it converts trigger pulses from up to 12 drum pads into MIDI information. The Drumslave also handles dynamics and features a high-hat pedal input.

MIDI Channelizer

This is a box for DX-7 fans. The Channelizer takes the DX-7 output (or the output from any other MIDI keyboard that transmits over channel 1), then tags on a new channel identification number so that MIDI information can be transmitted over any MIDI channel (1 through 16).

MIDI Channel Filter

Some synthesizers are stuck in Omni mode and will always listen to all signals coming in over all channels. If you want a synth to respond only to MIDI information coming in on one specific channel, the MIDI Channel Filter receives MIDI info and filters out all channels except for the one you select (which can be any one of the 16 basic channels).

MIDI Lighting Controller

This unusual box interfaces stage lighting to a MIDI system, thus allowing a totally synchronized audio-visual experience. As you operate the unit's lighting faders in time with a MIDI sequencer, the sequencer translates the fader settings into note messages and records this data into memory. On playback the data plays back through the Lighting Controller, which provides suitable control signals for most commercially-available dimmer packs.

MIDI Wind Driver

The Wind Driver (designed specifically to work with the Lyricon breath controller for synthesizer) translates pitch, envelope, and gate signals into a format suitable for use with MIDI equipment. Other pitch-to-voltage interfaces, such as those used to connect guitars and other instruments to CV/gate-oriented synthesizers, are also generally compatible with the Wind Driver.

Chapter 9

The Future of MIDI

MIDI is still, relatively speaking, brand new. Every few months someone comes up with a new way to use MIDI; before June 1985 there were no MIDI echo units . . . one month later there were about a half dozen.

MIDI's future is yet to be played out, and many of its effects are still to be felt. One possibility is that MIDI combined with inexpensive synthesizers, will draw more and more people who are not professional musicians into playing music. It's more gratifying to play an instrument than a record or CD, and with synthesizers the process of playing an instrument has become simpler. Throw in a drum machine, a home computer interface, and some software; and even people who thought they could never play an instrument will be able to enjoy themselves musically.

MIDI will surely change the face of recording as well: the MIDI sequencer has already started the process. As sampling machines improve, we might well see the end of the tape recorder as we know it today. Studios will have to adjust their way of doing business in order to survive in such a rapidly changing musical milieu, since musicians will be loathe to pay for doing overdubs in a studio when they can just as easily work out many of their parts at home.

An interesting side effect of MIDI is the role of the small manufacturer. When the musical instrument business consisted of non-compatible devices, it was impossible to create a product such as a general-purpose sequencer; each proprietary device required its own kind of proprietary accessory. If a small company came up with a product for one particular machine, then if the machine's manufacturer went out of business the small company did too. Thanks to MIDI, the accessory that works with one manufacturer's machine will work with any other manufacturer's machine (assuming that it follows the

MIDI specification). This means that smaller companies that put a substantial amount of time and money into creating a product are assured of a fairly broad market. The dozens of small software companies that sell MIDI-compatible products are essentially MIDI's first children.

Telecommunications will play an ever-increasing role in MIDI. We already have software-of-the-month clubs, where you receive a diskette, cassette, or RAM cartridge every month; the next step is to simply call up the "club," download programs into your machine via a modem, and charge the whole thing to a credit card. Some manufacturers are already discussing the option of creating "electronic bulletin boards" for owners. By using a modem to contact the bulletin board, users of that manufacturer's equipment will find out about software updates, news, and tips, and be able to download new programs or software.

One very encouraging sign is that manufacturers are continuing to work together to allow the MIDI spec to evolve in an intelligent, controlled way. MIDI is all about communications between equipment, which requires good communications (a very rare thing in this world) between all the people involved in making MIDI products. So far, manufacturers have shown an extraordinary ability to work together; and there's every reason to believe this will continue in the future.

And what about those two extra pins on the MIDI connector? Who knows . . . there have been rumors about a MIDI II spec in the works, but everything I've heard indicates this will not be ready for some time. In any event, it will supposedly be downward compatible with existing MIDI gear (in other words, current MIDI gear will work with MIDI II gear, but MIDI II gear will not necessarily work with current MIDI gear). And while we're speculating, what about all these computers that are springing up with built-in MIDI ports? There have been rumors that since MIDI is so inexpensive and simple, computer companies might use it for controlling more than just musical instruments (MIDI light dimmers, anyone?).

MIDI is here to stay, and I'm glad: it has a lot of potential. I hope this book has conveyed not only what MIDI is about, but some of my enthusiasm for what MIDI can do. Now go out there, patch some things together, study your gear, and have fun . . . 'cause that's what MIDI is *really* all about.

Appendix A

The MIDI Specification

The following public-domain document is reprinted with permission from

Sequential Circuits, Inc.
3051 North First Street
San Jose, California 95134

Document No. MIDI-1.0
Date: August 5, 1983

MIDI 1.0 SPECIFICATION

Introduction

MIDI is the acronym for Musical Instrument Digital Interface.

MIDI enables synthesizers, sequencers, home computers, rhythm machines, etc. to be interconnected through a standard interface.

Each MIDI-equipped instrument usually contains a receiver and a transmitter. Some instruments may contain only a receiver or transmitter. The receiver receives messages in MIDI format and executes MIDI commands. It consists of an optoisolator, Universal Asynchronous Receiver-Transmitter (UART), and other hardware needed to perform the intended functions. The transmitter originates messages in MIDI format, and transmits them by way of a UART and line driver.

The MIDI standard hardware and data format are defined in this specification.

Conventions

Status and Data bytes given in Tables I through VI are given in binary.

Numbers followed by an "H" are in hexadecimal.

All other numbers are in decimal.

Hardware

The interface operates at 31.25 (+/- 1%) Kbaud, asynchronous, with a start bit, 8 data bits (D0 to D7) and stop bit. This makes a total of 10 bits for a period of 320 microseconds per serial byte.

Circuit: See Figure 1. 5 mA current loop type. Logical 0 is current ON. One output shall drive one and only one input. The receiver shall be optoisolated and require less than 5 mA to turn on. Sharp PC-900 and HP 6N138 optoisolators have been found acceptable. Other high-speed optoisolators may be satisfactory. Rise and fall times should be less than 2 microseconds.

Connectors: DIN 5 pin (180 degree) female panel mount receptacle. An example is the SWITCHCRAFT 57GB5F. The connectors shall be labelled "MIDI IN" and "MIDI OUT." Note that pins 1 and 3 are not used, and should be left unconnected in the receiver and transmitter.

Cables shall have a maximum length of fifty feet (15 meters), and shall be terminated on each end by a corresponding 5-pin DIN male plug, such as the SWITCHCRAFT 05GM5M. The cable shall be shielded twisted pair, with the shield connected to pin 2 at both ends.

A "MIDI THRU" output may be provided if needed, which provides a direct copy of data coming in MIDI IN. For very long chain lengths (more than three instruments), higher-speed optoisolator must be used to avoid additive rise/fall time errors which affect pulse width duty cycle.

Data Format

All MIDI communication is achieved through multi-byte "messages" consisting of

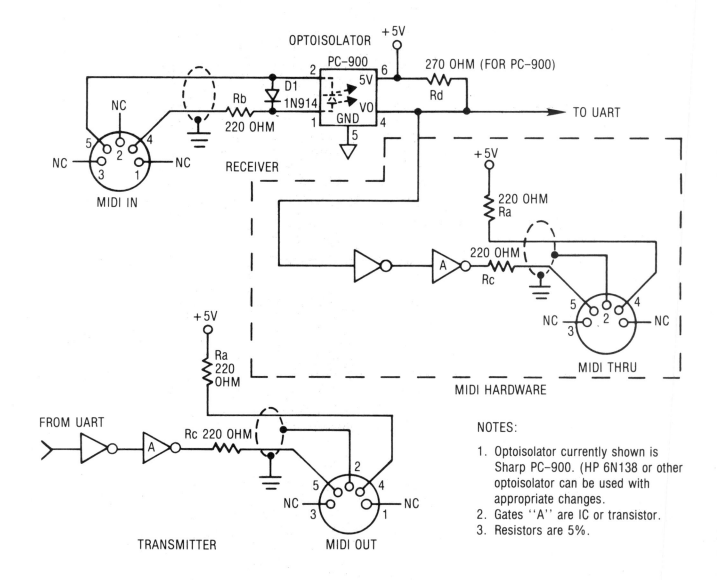

Figure 1. *MIDI Standard Hardware*

one Status byte followed by one or two Data bytes, except Real-Time and Exclusive messages (see next page).

Message Types

Messages are divided into two main categories: Channel and System.

Channel

Channel messages contain a four-bit number in the Status byte which addresses the message specifically to one of sixteen channels. These messages are thereby intended for any units in a system whose channel number matches the channel number encoded into the Status byte.

There are two types of Channel messages: Voice and Mode.

Voice. To control the instrument's voices, Voice messages are sent over the Voice Channels.

Mode. To define the instrument's response to Voice messages, Mode messages are sent over the instrument's Basic Channel.

System

System messages are not encoded with channel numbers.

There are three types of System messages: Common, Real-Time, and Exclusive.

Common. Common messages are intended for all units in a system.

Real-Time. Real-Time messages are intended for all units in a system. They contain Status bytes only—no Data bytes. Real-Time messages may be sent at any time—even between bytes of a message which has a different status. In such cases the Real-Time message is either ignored or acted upon, after which the receiving process resumes under the previous status.

Exclusive. Exclusive messages can contain any number of Data bytes, and are terminated by an End of Exclusive (EOX) or any other Status byte. These messages include a Manufacturer's Identification (ID) code. If the receiver does not recognize the ID code, it should ignore the ensuing data.

So that other users can fully access MIDI instruments, manufacturers should publish the format of data following their ID code. Only the manufacturer can update the format following their ID.

Data Types

Status Bytes

Status bytes are eight-bit binary numbers in which the Most Significant Bit (MSB) is set (binary 1). Status bytes serve to identify the message type, that is, the purpose of the Data bytes which follow the Status byte.

Except for Real-Time messages, new Status bytes will always command the receiver to adopt their status, even if the new Status is received before the last message was completed.

Running Status. For Voice and Mode messages *only*, when a Status byte is received and processed, the receiver will remain in that status until a different Status byte is received. Therefore if the same Status byte would be repeated, it may (optionally) be omitted so that only the correct number of Data bytes need be sent. Under Running Status, then, a complete message need only consist of specified Data bytes sent in the specified order.

The Running Status feature is especially useful for communicating long strings of Note On/Off messages, where "Note On with Velocity of 0" is used for Note Off. (A separate Note Off Status byte is also available.)

Running Status will be stopped when any other Status byte intervenes, except that Real-Time messages will only interrupt the Running Status temporarily.

Unimplemented Status. Any Status bytes received for functions which the receiver has not implemented should be ignored, and subsequent data bytes ignored.

Undefined Status. Undefined Status bytes must not be used. Care should be taken to prevent illegal messages from being sent during power-up or power-down. If undefined Status bytes are received, they should be ignored, as should subsequent Data bytes.

Data Bytes

Following the Status byte, there are (except for Real-Time message) one or two Data bytes which carry the content of the message. Data bytes are eight-bit binary numbers in which the MSB is reset (binary 0). The number and range of Data bytes which must follow each Status byte are specified in the tables which follow. For each Status byte the correct number of Data bytes must always be sent. Inside the receiver, action on the message should wait until all Data bytes required under the current status are received. Receivers should ignore Data bytes which have not been properly preceeded by a valid Status byte (with the exception of "Running Status," above).

Channel Modes

Synthesizers contain sound generation elements called voices. Voice assignment is the algorithmic process of routing Note On/Off data from the keyboard to the voices so that the musical notes are correctly played with accurate timing.

When MIDI is implemented, the relationship between the sixteen available MIDI channels and the synthesizer's voice assignment must be defined. Several Mode messages are available for this purpose (see Table III). They are Omni (On/Off), Poly, and Mono. Poly and Mono are mutually exclusive, i.e., Poly Select disables Mono, and vice versa. Omni, when on, enables the receiver to receive Voice messages in all Voice Channels without discrimination. When Omni is off, the receiver will accept Voice messages from only the selected Voice Channel(s). Mono, when on, restricts the assignment of Voices to just one voice per Voice Channel (Monophonic). When Mono is off (=Poly On), any number of voices may be allocated by the Receiver's normal voice assignment algorithm (Polyphonic).

For a receiver assigned to Basic Channel "N," the four possible modes arising from the two Mode messages are:

Mode	Omni	
1	On	Poly Voice messages are received from all Voice Channels and assigned to voices polyphonically.
2	On	Mono Voice messages are received from all Voice Channels, and control only one voice, monophonically.
3	Off	Poly Voice Messages are received in Voice Channel N only, and are assigned to voices polyphonically.
4	Off	Mono Voice messages are received in Voice Channels N thru N+M−1, and assigned monophonically to voices 1 thru M, respectively. The number of voices M is specified by the third byte of the Mono Mode Message.

Four modes are applied to transmitters (also assigned to Basic Channel N). Transmitters with no channel selection capability will normally transmit on Basic Channel 1 (N=0).

Mode	Omni	
1	On	All voice messages are transmitted in Channel N.
2	On	Mono Voice messages for one voice are sent in Channel N.
3	Off	Poly Voice messages for all voices are sent in Channel N.
4	Off	Mono Voice messages for voices 1 thru M are transmitted in Voice Channels N thru N+M−1, respectively. (Single voice per channel)

A MIDI receiver or transmitter can operate under one and only one mode at a time. Usually the receiver and transmitter will be in the same mode. If a mode cannot be honored by the receiver, it may ignore the message (and any subsequent data bytes), or it may switch to an alternate mode (usually Mode 1, Omni on/Poly).

Mode messages will be recognized by a receiver only when sent in the Basic Channel to which the receiver has been assigned, regardless of the current mode. Voice messages may be received in the Basic Channel and in other channels (which are all called Voice Channels), which are related specifically to the Basic Channel by the rules above, depending on which mode has been selected.

A MIDI receiver may be assigned to one or more Basic Channels by default or by user control. For example, an eight-voice synthesizer might be assigned to Basic Channel 1 on power-up. The user could then switch the instrument to be configured as two four-voice synthesizers, each assigned to its own Basic Channel. Separate Mode messages would then be sent to each four-voice synthesizer, just as if they were physically separate instruments.

Power-up Default Conditions

On power-up all instruments should default to Mode #1. Except for Note On/Off status, all Voice messages should be disabled. Spurious or undefined transmissions must be suppressed.

TABLE I

SUMMARY OF STATUS BYTES

STATUS D7—D0	# OF DATA BYTES	DESCRIPTION
Channel Voice Messages		
1000nnnn	2	Note Off event
1001nnnn	2	Note On event (velocity=0 Note Off)
1010nnnn	2	Polyphonic key pressure/aftertouch
1011nnnn	2	Control change
1100nnnn	1	Program change
1101nnnn	1	Channel Pressure (Aftertouch)
1110nnnn	2	Pitch wheel change
CHANNEL MODE MESSAGES		
1011nnnn	2	Selects Channel Mode
SYSTEM MESSAGES		
11110000	******	System Exclusive
11110sss	0 to 2	System Common
11111ttt	0	System Real Time

NOTES:

nnnn:	N—1, where N = Channel #, i.e. 0000 is Channel 1. 0001 is Channel 2. . . . 1111 is Channel 16.
*****:	Oiiiiiii, data, . . ., EOX
iiiiiii:	Identification
sss:	1 to 7
ttt:	0 to 7

TABLE II

CHANNEL VOICE MESSAGES

STATUS	DATA BYTES	DESCRIPTION
1000nnnn	0kkkkkkk	Note Off (see notes 1–4)
	0vvvvvvv	vvvvvvv: note off velocity
1001nnnn	0kkkkkkk	Note On (see Notes 1–4)
	0vvvvvvv	vvvvvvv≠0: velocity
		vvvvvvv=0: note off
1010nnnn	0kkkkkkk	Polyphonic Key Pressure (After-Touch)
	0vvvvvvv	vvvvvvv: pressure value
1011nnnn	0ccccccc	Control Change
	0vvvvvvv	ccccccc: control # (0–121) (see notes 5–8)
		vvvvvvv: control value
		ccccccc=122 thru 127: Reserved. See Table III.
1100nnnn	0ppppppp	Program Change
		ppppppp: program number (0–127)
1101nnnn	0vvvvvvv	Channel Pressure (After-Touch)
		vvvvvvv: pressure value
1110nnnn	0vvvvvvv	Pitch Wheel Change LSB (see note 10)
	0vvvvvvv	Pitch Wheel Change MSB

Notes for Table II on the following page.

NOTES:

1. nnnn: Voice Channel # (1–16, coded as defined in Table I notes)

2. kkkkkkk: note # (0–127)
   kkkkkkk=60: Middle C of keyboard

	0	12	24	36	48	60	72	84	96	108	120	127
			c	c	c	c	c	c	c	c		

   _____ piano range _____

3. vvvvvvv: key velocity
   A logarithmic scale would be advisable.

	0	1			64				127
	off	ppp	pp	p	mp	mf	f	f	fff

   vvvvvvv=64: in case of no velocity sensors
   vvvvvvv=0: Note Off, with velocity=64

4. Any Note On message sent should be balanced by sending a Note Off message for that note in that channel at some later time.

5. ccccccc: control number

ccccccc	Description
0	Continuous Controller 0 MSB
1	Continuous Controller 1 MSB (MODULATION WHEEL)
2	Continuous Controller 2 MSB
3	Continuous Controller 3 MSB
4–31	Continuous Controller 4–31 MSB
32	Continuous Controller 0 LSB
33	Continuous Controller 1 LSB (MODULATION WHEEL)
34	Continuous Controller 2 LSB
35	Continuous Controller 3 LSB
36–63	Continuous Controller 4–31 LSB
64–95	Switches (On/Off)
96–121	Undefined
122–127	Reserved for Channel Mod message (see Table III).

6. The controllers are not specifically defined. A manufacturer can assign the logical controllers to physical ones as necessary. The controller allocation table must be provided in the user's operation manual.

7. Continuous controllers are divided into Most Significant and Least Significant Bytes. If only seven bits of resolution are needed for any particular controllers, only the MSB is sent. It is not necessary to send the LSB. If more resolution is needed, then both are sent, first the MSB, then the LSB. If only the LSB has changed in value, the LSB may be sent without re-sending the MSB.

8. vvvvvvv: control value (MSB)
   (for controllers)

	0		127
	min		max

   (for switches)

	0		127
	off		on

   Numbers 1 through 126, inclusive, are ignored.

9. Any messages (e.g. Note On), which are sent successively under the same status, can be sent without a Status byte until a different Status byte is needed.

10. Sensitivity of the pitch bender is selected in the receiver. Center position value (no pitch change) is 2000H, which would be transmitted EnH-00H-40H.

TABLE III
CHANNEL MODE MESSAGES

STATUS	DATA BYTES	DESCRIPTION
101lnnnn	0ccccccc 0vvvvvvv	Mode Messages
		ccccccc=122: Local Control vvvvvvv=0, Local Control Off vvvvvvv=127, Local Control On
		ccccccc=123: All Notes Off vvvvvvv=0
		ccccccc=124: Omni Mode Off (All Notes Off) vvvvvvv=0
		ccccccc=125: Omni Mode On (All Notes Off) vvvvvvv=0

		ccccccc=126: Mono Mode On (Poly Mode Off)
		              (All Notes Off)
		vvvvvvv=M, where M is the number of channels
		vvvvvvv=0, the number of channels equals the
		              number of voices in the receiver.

		ccccccc=127: Poly Mode On (Mono Mode Off) vvvvvvv=0 (All Notes Off)

NOTES:

1. nnnn: Basic Channel # (1-16, coded as defined in Table I)
2. Messages 123 thru 127 function as All Notes Off messages. They will turn off all voices controlled by the assigned Basic Channel. Except for message 123, All Notes Off, they should not be sent periodically, but only for a specific purpose. In no case should they be used in lieu of Note Off commands to turn off notes which have been previously turned on. Therefore any All Notes Off command (123-127) may be ignored by receiver with no possibility of notes staying on, since any Note On command must have a corresponding specific Note Off command.
3. Control Change #122, Local Control, is optionally used to interrupt the internal control path between the keyboard,

for example, and the sound-generating circuitry. If 0 (Local Off message) is received, the path is disconnected: the keyboard data goes only to MIDI and the sound-generating circuitry is controlled only by incoming MIDI data. If a 7FH (Local On message) is received, normal operation is restored.

4. The third byte of 'Mono' specifies the number of channels in which Monophonic Voice messages are to be sent. This number, "M," is a number between 1 and 16. The channel(s) being used, then, will be the current Basic Channel (=N) thru N+M−1 up to a maximum of 16. If M=0, this is a special case directing the receiver to assign all its voices, one per channel, from the Basic Channel N through 16.

TABLE IV
SYSTEM COMMON MESSAGES

STATUS	DATA BYTES	DESCRIPTION
11110001		Undefined
11110010		Song Position Pointer
	01111111	1111111: (Least significant) hhhhhhh: (Most significant)
11110011	0sssssss	Song Select sssssss: Song #
11110100		Undefined
11110101		Undefined
11110110	none	Tune Request
11110111	none	EOX: "End of System Exclusive" flag

NOTES:

1. Song Position Pointer: Is an internal register which holds the number of MIDI beats (1 beat = 6 MIDI clocks) since the start of the song. Normally it is set to 0 when the START switch is pressed, which starts sequence playback. It then increments with every sixth MIDI clock receipt, until STOP is pressed. If CONTINUE is pressed, it continues to increment. It can be arbitrarily preset (to a resolution of 1 beat) by the SONG POSITION POINTER message.

2. Song Select: Specifies which song or sequence is to be played upon receipt of a Start (Real-Time) message.
3. Tune Request: Used with analog synthesizers to request them to tune their oscillators.
4. EOX: Used as a flag to indicate the end of a System Exclusive transmission (see Table VI).

TABLE V
SYSTEM REAL TIME MESSAGES

STATUS	DATA BYTES	DESCRIPTION
11111000		Timing Clock
11111001		Undefined
11111010		Start
11111011		Continue
11111100		Stop
11111101		Undefined
11111110		Active Sensing
11111111		System Reset

NOTES:

1. The System Real Time messages are for synchronizing all of the system in real time.
2. The System Real Time messages can be sent at any time. Any messages which consist of two or more bytes may be split to insert Real Time messages.
3. Timing Clock (F8H)
   The system is synchronized with this clock, which is sent at a rate of 24 clocks/quarter note.
4. Start (from beginning of song) (FAH)
   This byte is immediately sent when the PLAY switch on the master (e.g. sequencer or rhythm unit) is pressed.
5. Continue (FBH)
   This is sent when the CONTINUE switch is hit. A sequence will continue at the time of the next clock.
6. Stop (FCH)
   This byte is immediately sent when the STOP switch is hit. It will stop the sequence.
7. Active Sensing (FEH)
   Use of this message is optional, for either receivers or transmitters. This is a "dummy" Status byte that is sent every 300 ms (max), whenever there is no other activity on MIDI. The receiver will operate normally if it never receives FEH. Otherwise, if FEH is ever received, it will expect to receive FEH or a transmission of any type every 300 ms (max). If a period of 300 ms passes with no activity, the receiver will turn off the voices and return to normal operation.
8. System Reset (FFH)
   This message initializes all of the system to the condition of just having turned on power. The System Reset message should be used sparingly, preferably under manual command only. In particular, it should not be sent automatically on power up.

TABLE VI
SYSTEM EXCLUSIVE MESSAGES

STATUS	DATA BYTES	DESCRIPTION
11110000	0iiiiiii · (0*******) · · · · (0*******)	Bulk dump etc iiiiiii: identification Any number of bytes may be sent here, for any purpose, as long as they all have a zero in the most isgnificant bit.
	11110111	EOX: "End of System Exclusive"

NOTES:

1. iiiiiii: identification ID (0-127)
2. All bytes between the System Exclusive Status byte and EOX of the next Status byte must have zeroes in the MSB.
3. The ID number can be obtained from the MIDI committee. See Table VII.
4. In no case should other Status or Data bytes (except Real-Time) be interleaved with System Exclusive, regardless of whether or not the ID code is recognized.
5. EOX or any other Status byte, except Real-Time, will terminate a System Exclusive message, and should be sent immediately at its conclusion.

TABLE VII
MANUFACTURERS' ID NUMBERS

Sequential Circuits, Inc.	01H
Big Briar	02H
Octave/Plateau	03H
Moog Music	04H
Passport Designs	05H
Lexicon	06H
Oberheim	10H
Bon Tempi	20H
S.I.E.L.	21H
Kawai	40H
Roland	41H
Korg	42H
Yamaha	43H

Appendix B

Why Is My MIDI Messing Up?

MIDI is a wonderful tool, but nothing's perfect . . . and that includes MIDI. Jim Wright, who has had a lot of experience in dealing with MIDI idiosyncracies, wrote this Appendix on MIDI speed and timing considerations.

MIDI Transmission Delays

It takes just under a millisecond to transmit the typical three-byte MIDI message (**note on**, controller, pitch bend, etc.). To speed things up, *running status* (which I'll get to in a minute) was invented.

Assume that you can play an eight-note chord on a master keyboard with all eight notes being played at exactly the same instant. It will still take MIDI five- to eight-thousandths of a second to transmit all the notes. The expander synth probably takes another few thousandths of a second to respond—add it all up, and you may or may not hear a noticeable delay on some of the notes. Since nobody can play eight notes at *exactly* the same instant, MIDI transmission delays themselves are effectively not a real factor (delays can still occur from keyboard scanning and synthesizer voice response times).

However . . . assume you recorded that chord on a sequence, auto-corrected to exactly the same click. Now add in a bass line and melody note. Then decide to use the sequencer to play back all your drum parts, instead of just synchronizing the drum unit to the sequencer.

When you try to play all of that back, you may have 10 or 12 distinct events all scheduled for the exact same click. Since it will take MIDI up to 12 milliseconds to transmit all of them, they aren't going to happen on the same click. With complex parts like this, transmission delays can start to get noticeable.

Unfortunately, it can also get a lot worse. Continuous controllers like aftertouch and pitch bend can spit out a *lot* of data in a very short time. If even one of the sequencer tracks has continuous controllers on it, they will get "sandwiched in" between the notes and drum beats that are musically more important. The sequencer may try to stuff two or three controllers between every note (or even more, when they're really dense). Suddenly, the 10 ms delay from the first note to the last note balloons out to 30 ms—and that you can *definitely* hear. Some keyboards (in particular, the DX-7) *always* send out aftertouch data, making it very easy to run into this problem—and also creating a golden opportunity for makers of MIDI filter boxes.

If you have recorded lots of controllers on several tracks in the same places, you can drive the poor MIDI line absolutely bananas. It may not be able to even send all of the data—which leads us into the dreaded MIDI choke.

MIDI Choke

MIDI choke happens when too much data gets stuffed through MIDI too fast. Sometimes there's just too much data to be transmitted through a single MIDI port, and a sequencer bogs down (symptoms of this include timing glitches, stuttering, and possible crashes—total loss of data—under extreme circumstances).

It's much more common for the little computers in the instruments to freak out when data starts flying thick and fast. Remember, the sequencer has only to send the data—the instrument has to figure out what the data means and what to do with it.

The instrument also has to generate envelopes, keep voices sounding, and do lots of other "housekeeping." So, MIDI synths all have internal "buffers," where they can park fresh data until they have a spare moment to deal with it.

Under MIDI Choke conditions, data piles up faster than the synth can deal with it, until at some point the buffer "overflows" (runs out of space). Any data coming over MIDI at that point just gets thrown away, since there's no place to put it. Because the data that's thrown away may include **note off** commands, you can get stuck notes and other dreadful effects. Most MIDI synths will turn off all the notes still sounding when their buffers overflow to keep this from happening, but it's still no fun at all when it does happen.

MIDI channel filters can often help a lot. When the problem is lots of busy channels coming out of a sequencer, a channel filter can keep a synth from seeing any channels except the one for which it is set. Theoretically this happens inside the synth anyway—but it does take time for the synth to decode the channel for every message and decide whether or not it should be followed. A channel filter can keep the synth buffer from filling up with messages that aren't intended for the synth in the first place. You may or may not have to filter out pitch bends and/or aftertouch as well.

Some sequencers provide *density filters* that let you reduce the amount of data used for a complete pitch bend or other set of controller events. This can change a bend made up of tightly-packed events into one that is audibly the same but made up of a lot fewer events, spaced further apart. This kind of "bender slenderizer" can prevent MIDI choking without losing the expressive qualities that made you go from organ to synthesizer in the first place.

Running Status

With running status the first (status) byte need not be sent all the time. If the next message has the same status, you can just send the two data bytes for it *without* resending the status byte. The MIDI receiver will remember what the last status was and will use that to understand the new message. With long streams of pitch bends (or other status words), this can let you pack up to 50 percent more data into the same amount of time (it also reduces transmission delays by the same factor).

So what's the catch? Well . . . not everything understands running status. Most newer products do, but even one exception can be too many if you bought one. Matters also become more complex under MIDI choke conditions—if a buffer overflows and data is lost, it can be a while before a new status byte is received. All the data before that new status byte must be thrown out (ignored), even if the buffer has recovered, because there is no way of knowing what the correct status should be for that data. Some keyboards use running status extensively—if you ever have a problem with them, you may have to turn them on and off to get them to send a new status byte.

Appendix C

Interpreting a MIDI Implementation Sheet

MIDI implementation sheets are fairly standardized and follow a four-column format. The first column, Function, lists the function under discussion (basic channel options, aftertouch, etc.). The second column, Transmitted, indicates whether a function is transmitted; the third column, Received, indicates whether that function can be received. The fourth column consists of remarks. Let's look at individual sections of a couple of different MIDI implementation sheets to see how this all works.

The DX-7 implementation sheet gives the control change (controller) information as follows:

Function		Transmitted	Received	Remarks
	1	o	o	Modulation wheel
	2	o	o	Breath control
	4	o	o	Foot controller
	5	x	o	Portamento time
Control	6	o	o	Data entry knob[a]
Change	7	x	o	Volume
	64	o	o	Sustain foot sw
	65	o	o	Portamento foot sw
	96	o	o	Data entry +1
	97	o	o	Data entry −1

[a] Only when master tune is selected by panel button

Of course, the full implementation sheets covers other functions; we're just looking at one section as an example. As with most implementation sheets, o indicates a Yes, and x means no. Therefore, controller 7—volume—can receive information volume data and react accordingly, yet does not transmit volume data to other instruments. Portamento time acts similarly, however all the other controllers can either transmit or receive data.

Now let's look at the note range information for Roland's JX-3P.

This means that the JX-3P can send out note information over the range of notes from 36-96. There are two categories for receive: the range over which the instrument can respond (in this case, 0-127) and the range of received note numbers whose voices are normally created by the receiver's sound generating elements (called the True Voice).

A MIDI implementation chart can provide a wealth of MIDI-related data, so look it over carefully as you shop for MIDI gear.

Function	Transmitted	Received	Remarks
Note #	36–96	0–127	
True Voice		36–96	

Appendix D

MIDI Organizations and Publications

Electronic Musician Magazine (2608 Ninth St., Berkeley, CA 94710) is edited by the author and contains several MIDI-related articles in virtually every issue. Articles range from MIDI basics, to applications, to do-it-yourself projects involving MIDI.

International MIDI Association (11857 Hartsook St., North Hollywood, CA 91607). This is an organization of manufacturers and end users; dues are relatively high, but you get an informative monthly newsletter.

Keyboard Magazine (20085 Stevens Creek, Cupertino, CA 95014) carries articles about keyboard-related aspects of MIDI.

MIDI Manufacturers Association (c/o RolandCorp US, 7200 Dominion Circle, Los Angeles, CA 90040) is composed exclusively of MIDI manufacturers. It defines and extends the MIDI specification.

Roland Users Group Magazine (c/o Roland-Corp US, 7200 Dominion Circle, Los Angeles, CA 90040) is a manufacturer's newsletter that contains a fair amount of MIDI-related tutorials.